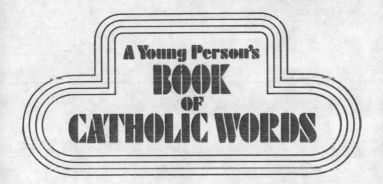

A Young Person's BOOK OF CATHOLIC WORDS

WILLIAM JACOBS

NAZARETH BOOKS
Doubleday & Company, Inc.
Garden City, New York
1981

ISBN: 0-385-17434-9
Library of Congress Catalog Card Number: 80-2078
Copyright © 1981 by The Catholic Heritage Press, Inc.
Printed in the United States of America
First Edition

Our Catholic heritage is tied to words. Christians are committed to words.

We learn our Faith through words. We express it in words. We usually pray in words. This is true even though much of religion is beyond words. For instance, we need words to explain symbols that express things that are hard to say.

In recent times, our heritage seems to have weakened, withered, almost died. It is, however, a long way from dead. One way to revitalize it is to know it well and communicate it well. That takes words.

Right now there is a lot of sloppy use of language and a poor appreciation of words and their usage. This book is intended to clarify and explain words of our heritage that come from Hebrew, Aramaic, Greek, and Latin roots, as well as being influenced by German or other languages.

One who masters the words in this book will not know all of religion. However, using this book, he or she should know it better and be able to talk and write about it more effectively.

Every attempt has been made to include the most important words, but no attempt has been made to give them more than their own meaning. Words alone cannot express faith, but they can help in the understanding of it. Understanding is essential to growth.

These are not "snob" or "in" words to set us apart. They are words that will help us understand where we came from, where we are going, and who we are.

We use words to bless. May the study of these words bless you. After all, they are all connected one way or another with the Word of God.

—William J. Jacobs
Saints Cyril and Methodius Seminary
1980

Notes to the User of The Book of Catholic Words:

+ Words or phrases printed in SMALL CAPITAL LETTERS are for the purpose of making cross-reference to other words defined in this book.

+ Pronunciation guide:
  Stressed syllables are marked with (′) unless all syllables in the word are of approximately equal stress

  A hard g sound is represented by a "g" as in the word God (gahd).

  A soft g sound is represented by a "j" as in the word angel (ayn′ · jell).

  A long "e" sound is represented by double letters "ee" as in the word almighty (all·my′·tee).

  Open vowel sound is represented by the vowel followed by an "h" as in the word water (wah·tur).

Other titles in the series:

A

abba

PRONUNCIATION: (ah'·bah)

A term found in Scripture referring to a way we can address the Father. It means "father" but in an especially childlike, intimate, and familiar sense—very much like "daddy."

absolution

PRONUNCIATION: (ab·so·lou'·shun)

Pardoning, taking away. In the sacrament of PENANCE (Sacrament of Reconciliation), we are absolved of our sins in order to be reconciled with God and the people of God. Through absolution, we are relieved of the effects of our guilt, at least in terms of eternal punishment.

abstinence

PRONUNCIATION: (ab'·stin·unse)

Refraining from certain food or drink. This is done as penance or simply to increase one's self-discipline. See FAST AND ABSTINENCE.

abundance

PRONUNCIATION: (ah·bun'·dunse)

Much prayer in and outside of the liturgy is asking for abundance, for example, abundance of crops. There is also abundance of life. Jesus said that he came so we may have life and have it more abundantly.

acolyte

PRONUNCIATION: (*ak'·oh·lite'*)

One who serves the priest at mass or other liturgical functions and may on occasion be asked to distribute Communion. This is officially a ministry given to men preparing for the priesthood, but it could be given to laymen. Others (usually young people) also perform such services, but they are called *servers* and normally do not distribute Communion unless commissioned for that. See EXTRAORDINARY MINISTER.

Acts of the Apostles

PRONUNCIATION: (*akts·uv·thee·uh·poss·ulz*)

A book of the New Testament that tells of life in the early Christian community.

Adam

PRONUNCIATION: (*ad·um*)

In Genesis, the first man created by God. Adam's sin brought ORIGINAL SIN on us all. Christ is called the New Adam because he came to destroy sin. *Adam* means "man," and some scholars believe that the name as used in Genesis could refer to a race or a nation. His mate was Eve in the Genesis account, and Adam blamed her for the Fall of humanity.

Adonai

PRONUNCIATION: (*ah·doe·nye*)

One of the names by which people have called God. It means "my lord." In the Jewish tradition, it was used as a substitute for YAHWEH, which was so holy as to be an "unspeakable name" of God.

Advent
PRONUNCIATION: {ad'·vent}
The season in which we prepare for Christmas. It calls for serious and prayerful preparation for Christ who is to come. We also use this time to prepare for the coming of God's kingdom and to make our lives more Christian today.

agape
PRONUNCIATION: {ah·gah·pee}
Derived from the Greek, roughly "love feast." A meeting in fellowship, as in the meals eaten together by the early Christians.

agnostic
PRONUNCIATION: {ag·nos'·tik}
One who doubts the existence of God. Such a person may be in real quest of truth. Agnostics who eventually embrace the Faith are often strong church members.

alb
PRONUNCIATION: {ahlb}
A long white garment worn by priests and other ministers during liturgy.

alleluia
PRONUNCIATION: {ah·lay·lou·ya}
A short hymn meaning "praise God." It is often found alone or at the end of several psalms in the

Old Testament (Psalms 105–107, 135) and in the Book of Revelation in the New Testament. It is usually left untranslated in the liturgy.

almighty
PRONUNCIATION: (all·my'·tee)
Having all power. In our tradition, we say that only God is Almighty.

alms
PRONUNCIATION: (ahmz)
Gifts of money or goods to the poor. Almsgiving is an ancient tradition in Judaism and Christianity, as well as in other religions. In our time, more than token giving is especially important.

alpha (A) and omega (Ω)
PRONUNCIATION: (al·fa·and·oh·may·guh')
The first and last letters of the Greek alphabet—the beginning and the end. The Hebrew people used these two letters to symbolize the vastness and timelessness of God. Christians have taken this tradition and applied it to Jesus Christ. In the Book of Revelation (1:8; 21:6; and 22:13), Jesus Christ is proclaimed as "Alpha and Omega . . . the beginning and the end."

altar
PRONUNCIATION: (all'·tur)
Originally a stone or pile of stones on which sacrifice or incense was offered. Later the altar became any place or structure where sacrifice or incense

10

was offered to God. In Jerusalem, the temple had an altar of bronze. Today our churches have altars that often look like tables (some of marble or other stone). The altars in our churches are designed to commemorate the table of the Last Supper and the one perfect sacrifice offered by Jesus to the Father. The altar is where the main action of the mass occurs.

amen

PRONUNCIATION: *(ah'·men'* or *ay'·men')*
Means "so be it," very definitely *yes*. It is a word that ends prayers, but more than anything it affirms what has been said during prayer. The Great Amen at the end of the Eucharistic Prayer of the mass expresses the community's wholehearted agreement with all that has been said.

Anamnesis

PRONUNCIATION: *(an·um·nee'·sis)*
The process of recalling. After the Consecration at mass, we recall the Paschal Mystery—the events in the life of Christ that brought about our salvation (life, death, Resurrection). The word is used in the narrative of the Eucharist in the New Testament (1 Corinthians 11:23–28; Luke 22:19).

angels

PRONUNCIATION: *(ayn'·jellz)*
In the Bible, the term usually means messengers of God appearing in some form that is higher than humanity because they are all spirit. Angels are able

11

to think and will to do things, but they have no bodies of flesh and bone. They are created, and of a higher order than human but less than divine.

annulment of marriage
PRONUNCIATION: (uh·null'·munt·uv·marr'·idge)
A declaration by a church court (tribunal) that the conditions of a valid, sacramental marriage did not exist in a particular case. It must be proved that a true marriage never existed. This leaves the parties free to marry.

Annunciation
PRONUNCIATION: (ah·nun·see·ay'·shun)
The feast on which we celebrate the announcement to Mary that she was to be the mother of Jesus. Reflection on this announcement is the first of the Joyful Mysteries of the Rosary.

anointing of the sick
PRONUNCIATION: (uh·noint·ing·uv·thuh·sick)
The SACRAMENT in which prayers are offered for the recovery of a person's health or as a preparation for death. It involves anointing with oils and remission of sin. The sacrament can be repeated.

anti-Semitism
PRONUNCIATION: (an·tee·sem'·uh·tizm)
Attitude and practice of hatred of Jews. It begins in prejudice (judging without enough knowledge and thought) and can end in serious discrimination, even violence.

apartheid

PRONUNCIATION: (ah·part'·hite)

Government policy of segregation of black and white people in the Republic of South Africa.

Apocalypse

PRONUNCIATION: (ah·pock'·ul·ipps)

The destruction of the forces of evil at the end of time. A name used for a book of the New Testament now called Revelation. See ESCHATOLOGY.

Apocrypha

PRONUNCIATION: (ah·pock'·ruh·fuh)

Writings in scriptural style sometimes claimed to be authentic parts of REVELATION but proved or considered false, or at least outside the realm of inspired writing.

apologetics

PRONUNCIATION: (ah·poll·oh·jett·iks)

An academic field that deals with defense and explanation of the Faith. For instance, it offers arguments for the divinity of Christ and the divine foundation of the church. The Latin word *apologeticus* means "defense, justification, presentation of evidence."

apostasy

PRONUNCIATION: (ah·poss'·tuh·see)

Formal denial or rejection of the Faith. An *apostate* turns completely against the church. In early Christianity there was an argument about readmis-

13

sion of apostates to the church. Now, an apostate who seriously wishes to repent and return can do so.

apostle
PRONUNCIATION: *(ah·poss'·ull)*
One who is sent, given a mission. A term for the twelve early church leaders chosen by Christ. Also a term for anyone in the church who accepts the task of carrying Christ's word and work to others.

apostolic
PRONUNCIATION: *(ap·pus·tahl'·ik)*
Having to do with the apostles. That is, apostolic teaching, apostolic succession of bishops, or apostolic works. In apostolic works we share in the mission of the apostles who were sent to teach and minister in the name of Christ.

apostolic delegate
PRONUNCIATION: *(ap·pus·tahl'·ik·del·uh·gate)*
A person whom the pope delegates to a country that does not have regular diplomatic relations with the Vatican (for instance, the United States). Similar delegates who also have diplomatic privileges are called *nuncios.*

apostolic succession
PRONUNCIATION:
(ap·pus·tahl'·ik·suck·sesh'·un)
Our tradition that all the bishops of the church follow in direct line from the apostles, and that the pope is the successor of Peter. Ordained bishops in

the early church passed on their office to others, and so on through history. This means that bishops have the power to teach, rule, and sanctify in the name of Jesus; and to ordain priests, deacons, etc. Bishops are full pastors of the territory to which they are assigned.

apparitions of the Lord
PRONUNCIATION: (ap·par·ish'·unz·uv·thuh·lord)
Appearances of Jesus, some in Scripture, some in private REVELATION

Ascension
PRONUNCIATION: (us·en'·shun)
The taking up of the risen body of Christ into heaven, the world of the divine. This was the final glorification of Jesus after he rose from the dead.

ashes
PRONUNCIATION: (ashuz)
In liturgy, a symbol of penance. Also a reminder, as on Ash Wednesday, that we are dust and will return to dust. Penitents in the early church appeared publicly in sackcloth and ashes to show their willingness to change from sin.

assembly
PRONUNCIATION: (uh·sem'·blee)
A gathering of people, used in the church in a generally solemn sense. At mass, the priest is president (presides over) the assembly of the people of God.

Assumption

PRONUNCIATION: *(us·sump'·shun)*

The doctrine that Mary was assumed into heavenly glory at the end of her life on earth. We celebrate Mary's Assumption on August 15.

atheist

PRONUNCIATION: *(ay'·thee·ust)*

One who does not believe in God. A militant atheist is one who actively opposes belief in God and participation in religious activities.

authoritative

PRONUNCIATION: *(uh·thor'·uh'·tay·tive)*

Spoken, written, or taught with official backing. For instance, official church or government pronouncements.

B

baptism

PRONUNCIATION: *(bap'·tizum)*

The SACRAMENT through which one becomes a Christian. By baptism one is initiated into the Church, incorporated into the BODY OF CHRIST, and freed from ORIGINAL SIN and all other sin. It is a new birth necessary for the reception of all the other sacraments.

beatific vision

PRONUNCIATION: (*bee·uh·tiff'·ik·vizh'·un*)

A way of stating the eternal happiness of heaven. Those in heaven behold God "face-to-face" and contemplate God's glory.

Beatitudes

PRONUNCIATION: (*bee·at·uh·toodz*)

Derived from the word *blessed*, which means "happy." These are the things Jesus said during the Sermon on the Mount, as related by Matthew and Luke. Blessed are the poor in spirit, the gentle, those who mourn, those who hunger and thirst for justice, the merciful, the pure of heart, the peace-makers, and those who are persecuted for Christ.

belief

PRONUNCIATION: (*bee·leef'*)

Something one holds to be true without need for scientific demonstration. That is, we believe in God, the virginity of Mary, and other articles of faith. There is good reason for such belief, but it is based on faith rather than demonstrable proof.

Benedictine

PRONUNCIATION: (*ben·uh·dick'·teen*)

Religious communities and traditions based on the Rule of Saint Benedict. The way of life is monastic, spent primarily at work and prayer. During the Dark Ages, the Benedictines did much to preserve civilization. In recent times they have contributed to scholarship and have been especially active in promoting good liturgy.

Bible

PRONUNCIATION: (by'·bul)

From the Greek word for "book." Our Bible is actually a library consisting of many books. They are divided into the Old and New Testaments. The Catholic Church regards the Bible as the inspired Word of God, revealing part of sacred doctrine.

bioethics

PRONUNCIATION: (by·oh'·eth'·iks)

A discipline that studies developments in medicine and other life sciences and tries to develop norms and standards for moral application of scientific findings. It is a recent field, complicated, and extremely necessary.

bishop

PRONUNCIATION: (bish'·up)

A man who has received the fullness of the priesthood; one who governs, teaches, and sanctifies a people. He is assigned to a territory, called a DIOCESE. With the pope, bishops share in governing the whole church.

blessing

PRONUNCIATION: (bless'·ing)

Humanity blesses God by adoration and thanksgiving (Psalm 103:1,2). We can bless others by wishing them well or happiness (Matthew 5:44). Christians believe that God **can** bring about good through blessing. God blesses us with creation and the spiritual, mental, and physical gifts we need to live. We pronounce or "say" blessings on things, food, or people to consecrate or return them in thanks to God. Many examples of this type of blessing are in Jesus' miracles and in the example he showed at the Last Supper.

body of Christ
PRONUNCIATION: (*bod·ee·uv·kryst*)
Baptized Christians form the body of Christ, also called the *mystical body of Christ.* This is based on 1 Corinthians 12:12–27, in which Saint Paul teaches that all Christians have an essential role in the work of Christ. Some theologians prefer the term *body of Christ mystically united.* In any case, we belong.

book of the gospels
PRONUNCIATION: (*book'·uv·thuh·gos'·pulz*)
This book contains only the gospel texts from which the DEACON proclaims the gospel of the day.

born again
PRONUNCIATION: (*born·uh·gen*)
Baptism is a new birth by ancient tradition. In recent times, the term *born again* has been used in some Protestant sects for one who has found personal salvation by accepting Christ and thus being born to new life.

bread and wine

PRONUNCIATION: (bred·and·wyne)

The stuff of life. Products of nature and human hands which become in liturgy the Body and Blood of Christ.

Bread of Life

PRONUNCIATION: (bred·uv·lyfe)

A reference to the Eucharist; the flesh of Jesus given us for the "life of the world." (John 6:51)

breaking of the bread

PRONUNCIATION: (bray·king·uv·thuh·bred)

When the priest breaks the bread in the mass, we recall the gesture of Jesus at the Last Supper when he broke bread and gave it to his disciples. In breaking the bread the church calls to mind that we who are many are made one in Jesus Christ who is our bread of life.

breviary

PRONUNCIATION: (brev'·ee·air·ee)

A book that contains the DIVINE OFFICE. The office is also known as the *Liturgy of the Hours*.

brothers of the lord

PRONUNCIATION: (bruh·thurz·uv·thuh·lord)

Persons who are generally around Jesus. They are often considered relatives or "cousins" of Jesus. James, Jude, Joseph, and Simon were among those referred to in Scripture as brothers of the Lord. Since, according to tradition, Jesus was Mary's only child, we generally see this term as meaning "cousin" (see Mark 6:1–6).

C

calumny
PRONUNCIATION: (kal'·um·nee)
Making untrue accusations against another person.

canonization of saints
PRONUNCIATION:
(kan·un·iz·ay'·shun·uv·sayntz')
Official proclamation by which the church declares a person to be among the saints in heaven. In modern and recent times, this proclamation comes only after long study of the person's life.

canon law
PRONUNCIATION: (kan·un·law)
The formally organized laws of the church, known as *canons*. They cover the following: administration of the sacraments, rights of persons, general government of the church, and penalties for serious violations.

Canon of Catholicity
PRONUNCIATION:
(kan·un·uv·kath'·ul·liss'·it·ee)
One must take the greatest possible care to believe what has been believed everywhere. This standard

for Catholic teaching and belief was stated by Vincent of Lerins in A.D. 434. It is a guide to the approach we should use in seeking out true DOGMA. The care involved should be equal to the care one has for one's own salvation.

capital punishment

PRONUNCIATION: {kap'·it·ul·pun'·ish·munt}
Punishing a criminal or other offender by killing him. Capital punishment has been considered moral by the state, and even in some cases by the church through the state. There is growing opinion, though, that executions do not serve justice, that they may be unjust, and that they are certainly not morally required. A Catholic is free to form a personal opinion about this issue, but such an opinion should be formed with great care.

cardinal

PRONUNCIATION: {kard'·in·ul}
A bishop who has been elevated to high rank and who is consulted on affairs of the church at the highest level. The cardinals as a body are known as the College of Cardinals. The official garb of a cardinal is red in color.

cardinal virtues

PRONUNCIATION: {kard'·in·ul·vir'·chooz}
PRUDENCE, JUSTICE, fortitude, and temperance.
Prudence: the habits and patterns we develop to help us choose God's will.
Justice: the desire and choice to be fair with others and ourselves.

Fortitude: the habit of not letting our fears get in the way of what we believe we should do.

Temperance: the habit we develop so we know the difference between what we need and what we want; being able to know when we have enough.

catechism

PRONUNCIATION: (kat·ik'·ism)

A book containing religious instruction. The best known in our country is the Baltimore Catechism, which had editions for various age levels. Usually such books followed a question-and-answer form. The Baltimore Catechism was widely used until Vatican II.

catechumenate

PRONUNCIATION: (kat'·uh·kew'·muh·nit)

Catechumens are adult converts who are preparing for reception into the church. In ancient times the catechumenate was a formal period of preparation for BAPTISM. Recently, a similar practice has been used to assure a more thorough and meaningful instruction of new members.

catholic

PRONUNCIATION: (kath'·uh'·lick)

Universal; worldwide; everywhere at all times.

celebrant's chair

PRONUNCIATION: (sell·uh·brentz·chayr)

The place where the priest who presides at the celebration of mass sits. It expresses his office of presiding over the assembly of believers gathered and his willingness to lead those present in prayer.

celebrate

PRONUNCIATION: (*sell·uh·brayt*)

To mark a solemn occasion with festivities. We celebrate not only mass, but all the sacraments, including penance. In these celebrations, there should be a characteristic of rejoicing which is often hard to observe in our liturgy.

celibacy

PRONUNCIATION: (*sell'·uh·biss·ee'*)

The church discipline through which priests voluntarily give up the rights and privileges of marriage. The law of celibacy could be changed, but this does not appear likely in the near future. The pope can make exceptions, that is, he can ordain married men, but such cases are rare.

centurion

PRONUNCIATION: (*sen·chur'·ee·on*)

Originally an officer of the legionnaires of Palestine. This person was in charge of one hundred men (a century), which was one-sixtieth of a Roman legion (six thousand men).

chalice

PRONUNCIATION: (*chal·iss*)

The chalice, or cup, has been both the symbol of divine blessing and of great trial. Since the Last Supper, in which the chalice was seen as the "cup of salvation," it has become the symbol of the Eucharistic Mystery (see 1 Corinthians 10:21). In Psalm 16, verses 5–6, the cup or chalice symbolizes humanity's call to be one with God.

chaplain

PRONUNCIATION: *(chap'·lin)*

One who represents the church in a prison, a hospital, an institution, or the armed forces. Usually a chaplain is an ordained clergyman, but recently religious men and women and some lay persons have become active and valuable in this work.

charism

PRONUNCIATION: *(kar·izm')*

A special gift of God to a person enabling that person to act more effectively in building up the body of Christ. This includes preaching, teaching, ministry of various forms, and other gifts. Such activity of the Holy Spirit is of the greatest importance, and it demands understanding and prudence. Any Christian can assume that God has given her or him grace for some special work in the church. There is nothing magical or mystical about it.

Charismatic

PRONUNCIATION: *(kar·iz·mat'·ik)*

A movement in the church that stresses the role of the Holy Spirit. It is marked by intense prayer and awareness of the Spirit's gifts. See PENTECOSTAL.

charity

PRONUNCIATION: *(char·uh'·tee)*

Means love. Charity is one of the THEOLOGICAL VIRTUES. It is necessary for salvation. Any sin violates charity because through sin we love God and man less than we should. It means more than giving ALMS.

chastity
PRONUNCIATION: (*chas'·tuh·tee*)
The choice to keep body, spirit, and mind in tune with the wishes of God as we understand them. The habit of keeping pure of mind, body, and spirit. See POVERTY, CHASTITY, OBEDIENCE.

chasuble
PRONUNCIATION: (*chaz'·yoo·bul*)
The outer vestment worn by a priest celebrating mass.

Chi-Rho
PRONUNCIATION: (*ky·row*)
Sometimes called *Christogram*. *Chi* (χ) and *Rho* (ρ) are the first Greek letters in *Christ* and are used as a symbol of Christ.

the Christ
PRONUNCIATION: (*thuh·kryst*)
A term for the Messiah who was to come, the Anointed One. We believe Jesus was the Christ.

Christian
PRONUNCIATION: (*kris'·chun*)
A follower of Christ. There is an interesting approach using the suffix *ian*. A beautician makes beauty happen; an electrician makes electricity happen; a physician makes health happen. A Chris-

tian makes Christ happen. This word was used for the first time at Corinth, Greece, about A.D. 35 as the term for the disciples of Jesus Christ. Up to that time, followers of Jesus were generally known as *Nazoreans* (see Acts 11:26).

Christian family

PRONUNCIATION: (*kris'·chun·fam'·ill·ee*)

In spite of current troubles in society, the church has usually taught that the family is society's basic unit. Christian marriage and the rearing of Christian children call for a special quality of family life marked by gratitude to God, appreciation of the sacredness of life, and service to humanity. Worship is special when families worship as families in the larger family of the church.

Christian initiation

PRONUNCIATION: (*kris·chun·in·ish·ee·ay'·shun*)

Entrance into the church by a new member through the sacraments of BAPTISM, CONFIRMATION, and the EUCHARIST. In early Christianity, the sacraments were received within a short time span in a formal process. This is again becoming more the case with new adult members. Confirmation of younger members close to or at the same time as baptism is the practice in some places.

church

PRONUNCIATION: (*churtch*)

The people of God with their hierarchical government make up what we call the Catholic Church.

By Vatican II teaching, we refer to Protestant and Orthodox groups as churches. The term is also used for a building that is a house of worship, but it should never be limited to this meaning.

Church year

PRONUNCIATION: (*churtch·yeer*)

Also called LITURGICAL YEAR. This is the calendar of sacred seasons and feasts. It begins each year with Advent and moves through a cycle that includes Christmas, Lent, Easter, and other seasons and events of church history. The cycle does not change, but individual dates may change from year to year.

ciborium

PRONUNCIATION: (*sy·bor'·ee·um*)

A container, often shaped like a cup or CHALICE with a cover, which is used to hold the consecrated bread for the distribution of communion.

cincture

PRONUNCIATION: (*sink'·tchur*)

A cord used as a tie at the waist and worn with liturgical vestments or with a religious habit.

circumcision

PRONUNCIATION: (*sir·come·sih'·shun*)

A surgical practice of removing the foreskin from the male sex organ. It is now common for health reasons. In ancient times it was a mark of being a Jew, but early Christians decided that new Christians who were not Jews did not have to be circumcised in order to enter the church. Jewish people still have a religious celebration when an infant boy is circumcised.

citizen
PRONUNCIATION: (sit·uh·zen)
One who is a resident and member of a nation or community and is entitled to protection from the community. We are citizens of Christ, we live in him, are members of him, and are promised protection by him.

cloistered nuns
PRONUNCIATION: (kloy·strd·nunz)
Communities of religious women who are isolated from the world in order to concentrate completely on prayer and contemplation. They include Carmelites, Poor Clares, some Dominicans, as well as other orders and communities. The church teaches that the value of this life is beyond our measure.

cloud
PRONUNCIATION: (klowd)
The cloud has been used to symbolize the presence of God. God's presence was seen on Mount Sinai (Exodus 19:9) in the form of a cloud, and in several other places in the Old Testament. In the New Testament, a cloud appears over Jesus at his TRANSFIGURATION (Matthew 17:5) and at his ASCENSION (Acts 1:9).

collegiality

PRONUNCIATION: (kull·ee·gee·al'·it·ee)

Shared authority in the church. The most common use of the term refers to the bishops governing with the pope, but it can be applied on lower levels.

coming

PRONUNCIATION: (kum·ing)

A translation of the Greek word *parousia*. In Matthew 23:3 and 1 Thessalonians 4:15, the word *coming* is used to designate the Second Coming of Christ for the Last Judgment.

commandment of love

PRONUNCIATION: (kum·mand'·munt·uv·luv)

Christ's command that we should love each other as he loves us. He loved us enough to live a full human life and to die for us.

commandments

PRONUNCIATION: (kum·mand'·munts)

The DECALOGUE. The Ten Commandments given to the people of God through Moses at Mount Sinai. (1) I am the Lord, thy God, thou shalt not have strange gods before me. (2) Thou shalt not take the name of the Lord thy God in vain. (3) Remember, keep holy the Sabbath Day. (4) Honor thy father and thy mother. (5) Thou shalt not kill. (6) Thou shalt not commit adultery. (7) Thou shalt not steal. (8) Thou shalt not bear false witness against thy neighbor. (9) Thou shalt not covet thy neighbor's wife. (10) Thou shalt not covet thy neighbor's goods.

commitment

PRONUNCIATION: *(kum·mitt'·munt)*

To entrust oneself to someone, to promise to do something or live in a particular way. We commit our lives to Christ. We should take our commitments to each other and to our work and service just as seriously because these are extensions of our commitment to Christ.

common priesthood

PRONUNCIATION: *(kom·mun·preest·hood)*

Also known as the *priesthood of the laity*. All Christians share in the priesthood of Christ through baptism and, through confirmation, are especially fitted for Christ's mission. This is different from the ordained priesthood of those who receive the sacrament of HOLY ORDERS. The common priesthood is no less important, and the ordained priest is not automatically superior. On the other hand, we teach that Christ acts often through the most unworthy priests.

Communion

PRONUNCIATION: *(com·mew'·nee·un)*

In the church this usually refers to reception of the Eucharist. It means "communication." In the Sacrament of the Eucharist, Christ communicates with us and is communicated to us as we are also drawn into communication with our fellow Christians. Thus, community is formed.

communion of saints

PRONUNCIATION: (com·mew'·nee·un·uv·sayntz)

The belief that there is active unity of persons on earth, in heaven, and in purgatory. Thus, we may ask those in heaven to pray for us, and we may pray for those in purgatory.

compassion

PRONUNCIATION: (kum·pah'·shun)

A virtue of sympathy with others. Compassion leads to action to aid people in their troubles.

confession of devotion

PRONUNCIATION:

(kun·fesh'·un·uv·dee·vo'·shun)

Reception of the sacrament of PENANCE when one is not aware of serious sin. The sacrament is received out of devotion to the forgiving Christ, with the hope that it will strengthen our bonds with him and with each other. The purpose is to receive the supernatural aid of the sacrament as well as the human benefits that come from facing our wrongs before another person. There is also the benefit of counseling, or spiritual direction. True conversion from sin is a long process. We need all the help we can get. See RITES OF PENANCE.

confessor

PRONUNCIATION: (kun·fess'·er)

A priest who is authorized to hear confessions and to celebrate the sacrament of PENANCE. It also means one who confessed or confesses the Faith. That means men and women who testify to the Faith even at the price of martyrdom at times.

confirmation

PRONUNCIATION: (kon·fur·may'·shun)

The SACRAMENT of confirmation completes Christian initiation. We teach that the Holy Spirit plays a special role in this sacrament. With reception of this sacrament, a person becomes fully a member of the church; faith has been confirmed.

conscience

PRONUNCIATION: (kon'·shuns)

The faculty by which we judge the good or evil of an action or omission in our lives. We have freedom of conscience and our conscience is the ultimate guide of our lives. The church provides special guidelines and tools to help form a truly free conscience. Great care is needed to form a good sensitive conscience.

consecrate

PRONUNCIATION: (kon'·suh·krayt')

To take an object from secular or worldly use and transfer it into sacred use or dedicate it to God's kingdom.

consecration

PRONUNCIATION: (kon'·suh·kray'·shun)

The part of the mass where the celebrant says the words Jesus said at the LAST SUPPER over the bread and wine. The bread and wine are thus consecrated as his Body and Blood to be sacrificed and shared in the Eucharistic Banquet.

Conservative Jew
PRONUNCIATION: (kun·serv·uh·tive·jew)
A Jew who follows some of the old rites and customs but is not nearly as strict as an ORTHODOX JEW. A Jew who includes a good amount of religious tradition in life and does not want to change anything in the Torah or in the ritual of Judaism. About midpoint between a REFORMED JEW and an ORTHODOX JEW, a Conservative Jew follows the dietary codes and other rules that the REFORMED JEW does not follow.

consistory
PRONUNCIATION: (kun·sis'·ter·ee)
A solemn assembly of the CARDINALS.

contemplation
PRONUNCIATION: (kon·tem·play'·shun)
A term referring to a mystical kind of union with God, usually through prayer. It can also refer to a more ordinary *gazing upon God* or reflecting on God and God's Word in a prayerful setting.

contrition
PRONUNCIATION: (kun'·trish'·un)
Sorrow for sin. The kind of sorrow that leads to forgiveness of sin should spring from love of God and regret for having failed to love God in our lives. Less perfect contrition is based on fear of punish-

ment or regret over the natural consequences of sin.

conversion
PRONUNCIATION: (kun·ver'·zhun)
Literally, "turning back to" or "turning around." This means more than non-Catholics joining the church. It applies to all of us who are called to a lifelong process of conversion to God. This is also known as *metanoia*, that is, deep spiritual change. In connection with repentance and penitence, conversion signifies total change of one's life. In Acts 2:38, the apostles called on their listeners to be converted and baptized. A popular use of the word *convert* is one who changes religions; however, the word never means that in the Bible.

Corpus Christi
PRONUNCIATION: (kor·pus·kris'·tee)
A Latin word which means Body of Christ. A traditional feast of great importance in the church.

Council of Chalcedon
PRONUNCIATION: (kown·sil·uv·kal'·suh·dun')
The council at which basic teachings on the humanity and divinity of Christ were developed. A.D. 451.

Council of Nicaea
PRONUNCIATION: (kown·sil·uv·ny·see'·uh)
The General Council at which the basic teaching on the Blessed Trinity was developed. A.D. 325.

Council of Trent

PRONUNCIATION: (kown·sil·uv·trent)

(1545–1563) The General Council that dealt with problems of the REFORMATION. Opinions and statements of Martin Luther and others were condemned. Disputed matters of doctrine and discipline were settled. The sacraments were defined and described precisely, their number fixed at seven.

covenant

PRONUNCIATION: (kuv·uh'·nunt)

An especially solemn contract or agreement, the greatest two being the Old Testament agreement between God and the Hebrew people and the New Testament agreement between Christ and his followers. Both express a relationship where God promises everything to those who lovingly obey.

covetousness

PRONUNCIATION: (kuv'·it·uss·ness)

Too great love or desire for things of the world at the expense of spiritual life.

creation

PRONUNCIATION: (kree·ay'·shun)

All that God has made. Our traditional belief is that God made the beginnings of our universe from nothing.

creator

PRONUNCIATION: (kree·ay'·tur)

Someone who can make something. The Creator is

36

God because only God has made something from nothing.

creed
PRONUNCIATION: (*kreed*)
A statement of belief. We express a summary of our faith by reciting a creed during liturgy. The best known is the Apostles' Creed, but there are others, such as that of Athanasius, which expressed the doctrine of the Trinity in great plainness.

cross
PRONUNCIATION: (*kross*)
Two beams or bars placed across each other to form an instrument of torture or execution.

crozier
PRONUNCIATION: (*kro'·zhur*)
The staff which a bishop carries when he presides at liturgy.

crucified
PRONUNCIATION: (*kru'·suh·fyde'*)
Nailed or tied hands and feet to a cross. We believe that Jesus was nailed to the cross, as is represented on a crucifix.

crucifix
PRONUNCIATION: (*kru'·suh·fix'*)
A carved or molded body (corpus) of Jesus on a cross. It may be of any size. The cross is probably the most universal sign of Christianity, and the crucifix is especially used by Catholics.

cruciform

PRONUNCIATION: *(kru'·suh·form)*

In the form of a cross. Many churches are designed in this form, which dates from medieval times.

culpable

PRONUNCIATION: *(kul'·puh·bull)*

Blamable. As used in morality, this means we can be blamed for an action in terms of how serious it is and how freely we acted in performing it. If we were forced to act, or acted without thinking, generally, we are not culpable.

cult

PRONUNCIATION: *(kult)*

A religious system and its followers. The term applies to Christianity and various groups within it. It can also apply to strange, fanatical groups. Also used popularly in a less formal sense. When RITUAL and MYTH merge, we have cult.

D

deacon

PRONUNCIATION: *(dee'·kun)*

The order of clergy below priest. There are two kinds of deacons. One will become a priest after a period of trial or training. The other is a permanent deacon who does not take vows of celibacy and therefore may be married. Deacons can baptize solemnly, give communion, preach, witness marriage, preside at burials, as well as assist in the eucharistic liturgy. The principal role of deacon is service to the people.

death
PRONUNCIATION: (*deth*)
In Catholicism, there are at least three senses of the term. One is bodily death, the end of earthly life. Another is spiritual death, meaning the loss of one's soul to the point of deserving hell. The third is a kind of death in spirituality: we die to sin and things that lead us away from God; in such dying, we find our life.

decade
PRONUNCIATION: (*deck'·aid*)
Anything that numbers ten, such as a period of ten years, or a decade of the rosary with its ten Hail Marys.

Decalogue
PRONUNCIATION: (*deck'·uh'·log*)
The Ten Commandments that are described in the Old Testament book of Deuteronomy, chapters 5 and 6. See COMMANDMENTS.

descendants
PRONUNCIATION: (*duh·send'·unts*)
Children of the same family. All people are seen as descendants or children of Adam and Eve.

descent of the Spirit
PRONUNCIATION: (*duh·sent'·uv·thuh·speer'·it*)
After Christ's Ascension, the coming of the Holy

Spirit on the apostles at Pentecost. This is considered the actual beginning of the church.

detraction

PRONUNCIATION: (*dee·trak'·shun*)

Damaging the reputation of another person by reporting things about him or her that are true, but needn't be made public. See REPUTATION.

devil

PRONUNCIATION: (dev'·ul)

There is reference in Scripture to the devil and also to devils. What is meant is an evil spirit. We can also simply see the idea of the devil as the spirit of evil in the world which leads us away from God. Whether the devil is an actual spiritual person has been argued, but no one can ignore the spirit of evil.

diakonia

PRONUNCIATION: (*dee·uh·ko'·nee·uh*)

A Greek word from which comes our title "deacon." It means service to the community. A deacon is called to serve the members of the community in their spiritual needs and other worldly needs including food, shelter, and companionship. In the Acts of the Apostles (6:1–6) the deacon brings alms to the poor.

dialogue

PRONUNCIATION: (*dye'·uh·log*)

Conversation among two or more persons, as in dialogue of a play. In religion, it is used in the sense of serious discussion of attitudes, opinions, and beliefs, for example, the Jewish-Catholic dialogue.

Diaspora

PRONUNCIATION: (dee·ass'·puh·ruh)

The scattering or dispersion of the Hebrew people during their exile after falling to their enemies. Prophets promised that a *faithful remnant* would remain. Recently the church has been said to be in a state of diaspora. If that is so, we should strive to be part of the faithful remnant, the small part that remains.

Didache

PRONUNCIATION: (did'·uh·kee')

Early instruction in the Christian community as reflected in a book probably written in the second century at Antioch. It is known as *The Instruction of the Apostles.*

diocese

PRONUNCIATION: (die'·uh·sis)

A territory of the church, similar to a state or county in civil government. Smaller territories within a diocese are called PARISHES.

discernment

PRONUNCIATION: (dis·ern'·ment)

An important term in moral choice and spirituality. Discernment means judgment and insight by which a person seeks to decide whether a course of action is correct in terms of her or his relationship with God.

disciple

PRONUNCIATION: (*dih·sipe'·ul*)

A follower who spreads a master's teaching, as did the disciples of Christ. A convinced member of a group or CULT.

discrimination

PRONUNCIATION: (*dis·krim·in·ay'·shun*)

Attitudes and practices that deny certain people or groups their rights. Anything that places a race, class, nation, or any group of people in a position to receive unfair treatment. Discrimination is a source of grave evil.

dispensation

PRONUNCIATION: (*dis·pen·say'·shun*)

An act by which a Catholic is freed from some rule or prohibition by a priest, by a bishop, or by the holy see. For instance, dispensation from fasting or dispensation for marriage to a non-Catholic.

divine nature

PRONUNCIATION: (*dih·vine·nay·chur*)

God's power and all God's perfection as we have come to know it.

Divine Office

PRONUNCIATION: (*dih·vine·awf·iss*)

Formal prayer recited or sung by priests and religious. Lay persons are urged to participate. The Divine Office consists of psalms, hymns, scriptural readings, and prayers.

divorce

PRONUNCIATION: *(div·orse')*

The church generally opposes divorce. Marriage is seen as a lifetime sacramental commitment. However, for very serious reasons—such as protection of a person's life or faith—separation may be approved. If civil divorce is necessary in order to settle legal problems of separation, the church does not object. However, the parties are not free to marry unless there is a decree of nullity (see ANNULMENT OF MARRIAGE).

doctor of the church

PRONUNCIATION: *(dok'·tur·uv·thuh·churtch)*

A title of great honor given to saintly teachers in the church.

doctrine

PRONUNCIATION: *(dok'·trin)*

A teaching of the church that is less formal than DOGMA, but still authoritative. Like dogma, it is proposed for belief.

dogma

PRONUNCIATION: *(dog'·muh)*

A statement of belief taught formally by the church as essential to the Faith. The body of formal essential teachings. Dogma is stated precisely, but it is open to clearer explanation and development.

doing penance

PRONUNCIATION: *(doo·ing·pen'·unse)*

In addition to performing PENANCE prescribed in the

sacrament, any fasting sacrifice or good works performed to show our sorrow for our sin. In ancient times penance often meant making direct amends to the person harmed or offended. By ancient tradition, this kind of penance can lead to great spiritual growth. It is often neglected in our time.

Dominican

PRONUNCIATION: (duh·min'·ee·kun)

The religious orders and traditions following Saint Dominic. Like the FRANCISCANS, the Dominicans combine contemplation and action. There is stress on intellectual activity. Saint Thomas Aquinas was only one of the many great minds of the church who was nurtured in the Dominican tradition.

dominion

PRONUNCIATION: (doe·min'·yun)

Having rule or power over someone or something. In religion, the rule of God over all creation. God extends this rule to the human race over the rest of earthly creation to bring order and make earthly life more fruitful as far as possible. God has dominion over humankind. We could be said to have dominion over earthly life. Wrong use of this power could cost us salvation.

dove

PRONUNCIATION: (duv)

In Matthew 3:16 we find this bird (of the pigeon family) used as a symbol because of its gentleness and purity.

drug abuse

PRONUNCIATION: (*drug·ah·bews*)

Catholics are taught that drugs, including alcohol, may be used to promote health. Moderate use of alcohol is not considered immoral. However, heavy use of any drug or alcohol can lead to sin. If we damage or abuse our bodies, we damage or destroy what God has made. In such abuse, we also damage our minds and spirits.

duty to forgive

PRONUNCIATION: (*dew·tee·to·for·give*)

Forgiveness is not an option for Christians, but a duty. We are to forgive others as God forgives us. This is often difficult, but it is close to the essence of being Christian.

E

Easter

PRONUNCIATION: (*ee·ster*)

The celebration of Christ's Resurrection from the dead.

Easter candle

PRONUNCIATION: (*ee·ster·kandl*)

Also known as the Paschal candle. It is lighted at the Easter Vigil and it represents the coming of the risen Christ as the light of the world. It remains lighted during all masses until Ascension.

ecclesia

PRONUNCIATION: (ek·klees'·ee·yuh)
A Latin word for "church."

ecclesial

PRONUNCIATION: (ek·klees'·ee·yul)
Having to do with the church.

ecclesiology

PRONUNCIATION: (ek·klees'·ee·ahl·oh·gee)
The study of the church, its history, structure and theology.

ecumenism

PRONUNCIATION: (ek·kew'·men·iz'·um)
The movement that seeks unity among divided Christians and works for improved relations with all non-Christian religions.

Eden

PRONUNCIATION: (ee·den)
The name that the Sumerians used for the earthly paradise. Eden has become a symbol of joy and happiness as seen in Genesis 2:15; a symbol of pain following the Fall of Adam and Eve; and a symbol of hope since the coming of Jesus Christ.

election

PRONUNCIATION: (ee·lek'·shun)
A term for God's choosing of a person or a people to fulfill a mission or way of life. As members of God's people, we are elected.

embolism

PRONUNCIATION: *(em'·bull·izm)*

This is the prayer which comes right after the Lord's Prayer in the mass. It develops the themes of the Lord's Prayer: deliverance from evil, the ability to live in peace, and turning of our will over to the care and understanding of our loving god.

Emmanuel

PRONUNCIATION: *(ee·man'·yew·ell)*

A name meaning "God with us." Applied to Jesus Christ.

Emmaus

PRONUNCIATION: *(ee·may'·us)*

A village situated about twenty miles from Jerusalem. On the evening of the Resurrection, Jesus appeared to two disciples who were on their way to Emmaus. (Luke 24: 13–35.)

encyclical

PRONUNCIATION: *(en·sick'·lee·kul)*

A letter written by a pope to teach faith, morals, or some aspect of the conduct of the church. Over the years, some of our most important teaching on worship, Scripture, ethical conduct, and human rights have come from encyclicals.

epiclesis

PRONUNCIATION: *(ep·uh·klee'·sis)*

That prayer in the mass in which the church calls upon the Holy Spirit. In this prayer we ask that the gifts we offer be consecrated, therefore becoming the body and blood of Christ who is the source of our salvation.

second epiclesis

PRONUNCIATION: (*sek'·und·ep·uh·klee'·sis*)
The time in the mass when the Holy Spirit is called upon so that the church may become and remain one body, one Spirit in Christ.

epiphany

PRONUNCIATION: (*ee·piff'·ah·nee*)
A manifestation or plain showing of something such as the glory of Christ. In the Catholic tradition, we celebrate the Feast of the Epiphany about twelve days after Christmas.

epistle

PRONUNCIATION: (*ee·pis'·ul*)
Literally "a letter," a collection of which makes up part of the New Testament. These are communications from Saint Paul and others to the early Christian communities. They contain theology as well as instruction on morality, prayer, and Christian life.

eschatology

PRONUNCIATION: (*ess·ka·tol'·oh·gee*)
A word traditionally meaning study and reflection on the "last things": death, judgment, heaven, and hell. In a broader sense, it means consideration of the mystery of what lies ahead when Christ will

come in glory. Its adjective form, *eschatological* (ess·kat'·oh·lod·gee·kul), is hard to say and spell.

Essenes

PRONUNCIATION: (ess·eenz')

A sect of Old Testament Jews of which many scholars believe John the Baptizer to be a member. The Dead Sea Scrolls seem to indicate that the Essenes were as important in the Jewish hierarchy as were the PHARISEES and Sadducees. There were about four thousand Essenes and about two hundred of them lived in Qumran. Much like our religious communities, the members of the sect had to undergo a one-year *postulancy* and a three-year NOVITIATE. Each member vowed to be reverent, to be just, to hate sin, to obey superiors, to tell the truth, to share all property and possessions, and to keep the Essene teachings secret.

eternity

PRONUNCIATION: (ee·turn'·it·ee)

Timelessness. Existence without beginning or end.

ethnic

PRONUNCIATION: (eth'·nik)

A term referring to the customs and practices of various national and racial groups. Within the church, we have ethnic parishes—Polish, German, Italian, etc. These are not as common as they were earlier in the century, but they express the richness and variety of our heritage as Catholics.

Eucharist

PRONUNCIATION: (yuke'·uhr·ist)

The central Sacrament of the church. Literally meaning "thanksgiving," the Eucharist is the Body and Blood of Christ, sacrificed in the mass, taken as nourishment by the faithful. It contains all the elements of the Paschal Mystery.

eucharistic community

PRONUNCIATION:
(yuke·uhr·ist'·ik·kom·mew'·nit·ee)

A term for any group that assembles around the Eucharist. Broadly applied, the eucharistic community refers to all who center their worship of Christ through the Sacrament of the Eucharist.

Eucharistic Liturgy

PRONUNCIATION: (yuke·uhr·ist'·ik·lit'·ur·gee)

Another term for mass, the principal act of worship of the church.

Eucharistic Prayer

PRONUNCIATION: (yuke·uhr·ist'·ik·prair)

The principal prayer of the mass, which includes the Consecration, as well as prayer for temporal things and for the dead, and ends with the words "Through him, with him and in him . . ." Since the Second Vatican Council, in the tradition of the early church, there are several forms of Eucharistic Prayer used at mass.

Eucharistic Sacrifice

PRONUNCIATION: (*yuke·uhr·ist'·ik·sack'·ruh· fyse*)

The church teaches that the Mass is not just a reenactment, but the actual, nonbloody sacrifice of the Body and Blood of Christ. His death on Calvary could only happen once, but its eucharistic representation is a prayer of universal meaning.

euthanasia

PRONUNCIATION: (*youth·an·ayzh'·uh*)

Mercy killing. Ending human life by the choice of a suffering person or that person's family. Although we may sympathize with apparent hopeless suffering, we cannot take it upon ourselves to be the ones who decide to directly end human life. See ORDINARY MEANS. Sometimes it is considered right to discontinue treatment that merely prolongs suffering and involves unnecessary pain and expense. This is different from mercy killing because nothing is actively done to end the person's life.

evolution

PRONUNCIATION: (*ev·oh· lew'·shun*)

A process of development. Darwin's theory of evolution holds that humanity descended from lower animal forms. However, the term can be used to describe anything that grows or develops; for instance, ideas or talents.

excommunication

PRONUNCIATION:

(eks'·ko·mew'·nuh·kay·shun)

Being officially cut off from the church because of some grave wrong. Today, there are fewer reasons for excommunication than in other times, and the church always wishes to restore the offender if that person repents. In a sense, we excommunicate ourselves whenever we commit serious sin, but the sacrament of PENANCE restores us to full Christian dignity.

exegesis

PRONUNCIATION: (eks·uh·jee'·sis)

Explanation or interpretation of Scripture. This is a difficult pursuit that requires long study. Relatively simple exegesis is found in most HOMILIES.

Exodus

PRONUNCIATION: (eks'·oh·duss)

The escape, led by Moses, of the Hebrew people from slavery in Egypt. The theme of the Exodus has many deep meanings within religion, the central meaning being our escape from the slavery of sin into new life with God.

extraordinary minister

PRONUNCIATION:

(ek'·stror·din·aree·mih'·niss·tur)

A person selected and officially designated to administer the Eucharist when there are not enough priests, or in other special circumstances. In other sacraments, an extraordinary minister may be a cleric who does not normally celebrate except in special circumstances. Often called MINISTERS OF COMMUNION.

F

faith

PRONUNCIATION: (fayth)

Belief based on the believability of the one proposing the belief. In other words, we believe what God has revealed because we are convinced that God can and must be believed. Faith calls for a life in which we try to act according to our beliefs. Faith is that free gift from God enabling us to believe in God as we understand God.

faithful departed

PRONUNCIATION: (fayth'·ful·dee·part'·ed)

Those who have died in the Faith and may be in heaven or purgatory. We pray for them at every mass and on other occasions.

faith healing

See HEALING.

false prophets

PRONUNCIATION: (fawls·prof·its)

From ancient times we have been warned against false prophets. We have been told that they would appear before the end of time in the form of appealing and highly skilled persons who would seem to bring holy messages but would be leading us away from God. The moral in this warning is that we must use great care to study or examine any new or unusual teaching or preaching. We must seek advice from wise persons before accepting any new form of holy teaching. On the other hand, we must be just as careful not to reject true prophets if they appear.

fast and abstinence
PRONUNCIATION: (*fast·and·ab'·stuh·nuhns*)
We fast, that is, we give up all or most food on some occasions, especially during Lent, as penance and in preparation for a feast. We abstain from meat on some days for the same reason. We refrain from eating or drinking anything but water or medicine (for one hour) in preparation for receiving the Eucharist. This is called the *Eucharistic fast*. Abstinence can also mean voluntarily avoiding alcoholic drink.

fasting
PRONUNCIATION: (*fast'·ing*)
Since early times fasting has meant complete abstinence from food. Those who fast may drink water. Fasting has always had a spiritual meaning. In recent times, the fasting of Martin Luther King for civil rights of American blacks and the fasting of Mahatma Gandhi for world peace have drawn attention to the needs of others. Fasting is a way to get out of one's self and become aware of the needs of others.

54

fathers of the church

PRONUNCIATION: (fah·thurz·uv·thuh·churtch)

A title given to saintly leaders of the early church who helped form Christian doctrine and guided Christian life. Most of these church fathers were bishops of the first eight centuries, although some were laymen and laywomen.

fault

PRONUNCIATION: (fawlt)

A human weakness or tendency to bad action. Faults in themselves are not usually sinful, but they can lead to sin if not checked.

fire

PRONUNCIATION: (fy·uhr)

In religious terms, fire is a symbol for the presence of God. For example, the Holy Spirit appeared "in tongues of fire." In the Old Testament, fire was a symbol of purification. We also speak of hell in terms of fire; however, the image of hell's fire does not have to be taken literally.

firstborn

PRONUNCIATION: (first·born)

By ancient Jewish tradition, every firstborn male must be reserved for God. The title firstborn was commonly given to the boy even if he had no brothers or sisters after his birth. By being firstborn, the child was given "birthright," which gave him the position of honor and a double share in the inheritance from his father. Jesus is often referred to as the firstborn of creation because of his position as the head of all humanity. (See Hebrews 1:6.)

forgiveness

PRONUNCIATION: (for·give'·ness)

Excusing a fault or offense. God forgives us if we forgive ourselves and one another. There must be forgiveness to have reconciliation—the renewing of a good relationship.

Franciscan

PRONUNCIATION: (fran·sis'·kun)

The religious orders and tradition following Saint Francis of Assisi. Within Franciscan orders there is great stress on poverty, works of mercy, and penance, as well as a combination of CONTEMPLATION and an active mission to the world.

fraternal correction

PRONUNCIATION: (fra·ter'·nul·ko·rek'·shun)

We are not to judge the moral worth of others. On the other hand, we have a Christian obligation to warn or caution others when we believe they are in spiritual danger because of something they say or do. This must be done with PRUDENCE.

free will

PRONUNCIATION: (free·will)

Liberty to choose the right thing or the wrong. Catholics believe that human beings have the intelligence to know what choices are appropriate, the free will to choose appropriate action, and the ability to take responsibility for those actions.

friar

PRONUNCIATION: (fry·uhr)

A member of a religious order who combines contemplation with action. A friar's work is usually outside the friary, in the world, and that is how his life differs from the life of a MONK.

fundamentalist

PRONUNCIATION: (fun·duh·men'·tul·ist)

One who takes a literal view of the Bible. A fundamentalist takes Scripture (in whole or part) to mean exactly what it says in terms of modern language and current usage. There is little in Scripture that can be taken this way. The church has consistently opposed fundamentalism, urging true study of the nature of the Bible and skilled interpretation of its contents.

G

genealogy

PRONUNCIATION: (gee·nee'·ahl'·ah·gee)

A list of one's ancestors. Genealogies appear frequently in the Bible. They are a means of showing from what family or tribe a person came. It is much like a birth certificate or social security number, for it identifies the person. Jesus, for instance, was of the line of David.

general absolution

PRONUNCIATION: (jen·er·ul·ab·so·lew'·shun)

For a number of serious reasons, a priest may give

all persons present absolution, forgiveness of their sins, and reconciliation with the church, without individual confessions. Generally, however, one is to confess any serious sin before receiving general absolution a second time. Church law requires that mortal sin be confessed privately before absolution can be received. The reason for this is not that the sins were unforgiven, but that the law demands confession.

General Council
PRONUNCIATION: (jen·er·ul·kown'·sil)
Also called Ecumenical Council. A gathering of bishops of the world with the pope to discuss Catholic life and belief and to develop teaching or practice.

genesis
PRONUNCIATION: (jen'·uh·sis)
The word means "beginning." The Book of Genesis, the first in the Old Testament, tells of the beginning of the world and of humankind.

Gentile
PRONUNCIATION: (jen'·tile)
A term used to indicate all non-Jewish peoples. Actually, goyim, translated "Gentiles," really means nations or peoples.

genuflection
PRONUNCIATION: (jen·yew·flex·shun)
Descending on one knee and arising as a sign of reverence before a great power or ruler. Thus, we

genuflect when entering a place where the Lord is present in the Eucharist.

gifts of the Spirit

PRONUNCIATION: *(gifts·uv·thuh·speer'·it)*
See CHARISM. Special gifts such as teaching, governing, doing pastoral work in an exceptional way, and saintly life are all for the building up of the BODY OF CHRIST.

gloria

PRONUNCIATION: *(glo'·ree·uh)*
An ancient hymn of praise in which the church prays to the Father. In the mass, it is used on all Sundays (outside of advent and lent) and on special feast days. The term gloria comes from the Latin phrase "gloria in excelsis deo" which is the first line in the hymn and is translated "glory to God in the highest." The first few lines of this hymn of praise are taken from the gospel account of St. Luke in which he describes the birth of Jesus.

glory

PRONUNCIATION: *(glor·ee)*
Honor, praise, magnificence. We speak of the glory of God and also of the glory awaiting us in heaven that is far greater than any earthly glory.

God

PRONUNCIATION: *(gahd)*
Our loving Father in heaven. The Creator of all things. The Supreme Being. See CREATION, TRINITY, YAHWEH, ABBA.

Golgotha

PRONUNCIATION: (gol·goth'·uh)

Place where Jesus was crucified. Called the *Place of the Skull* in Matthew 17:33.

Good News

PRONUNCIATION: (good·newz)

The term that led to our word GOSPEL as understood in English. The Good News is that Christ has come to bring salvation and victory over evil.

Gospel

PRONUNCIATION: (goss·pull)

The GOOD NEWS of Christ. God wills the salvation of all men and makes this possible through Christ. The four books of the Gospels (Matthew, Mark, Luke, John) represent the early Christian reflections on the life and teachings of Jesus.

grace

PRONUNCIATION: (grayss)

The free gift of God through Christ through which we know, share, and participate in God's love. Grace is thus an aid to Christian living and necessary for salvation.

grave sin

PRONUNCIATION: (grayve·sin)

A term more and more in use today, it means a serious offense that is less than deadly or MORTAL SIN but more than VENIAL SIN. Grave sin would call for thoughtful correction through the sacrament of PENANCE.

guilt

PRONUNCIATION: *(gilt)*

The fact of having committed an offense against the law. Guilt is also a term involving feelings of being guilty that are not necessary, either because the offense has been forgiven, has never occurred, or is long past. Such guilt can be dangerous to mental health.

H

habit

PRONUNCIATION: *(hab'·it)*

Any kind of behavior that becomes fixed by repetition. In other words, one who smokes a lot gets the habit of smoking. There are both good and bad habits which affect morality for better or worse. The term is also used for clothing worn by members of religious orders.

hate

PRONUNCIATION: *(hayt)*

An attitude or a sin in which we truly wish evil for another person or group of persons. There are many forms of hate and many degrees. It is always the opposite of love and is a main cause of sin, having destructive effects here and hereafter. A Christian gets angry sometimes and may dislike persons and things. That is human, although not perfect. However, one cannot truly hate and be truly Christian.

healing

PRONUNCIATION: (*heel'·ing*)

Bringing about recovery from physical, emotional, and spiritual disorders through prayer and spiritual purification. There has been great interest in this during recent years. Amazing results have been reported at times. The church approves such activity if practiced with discretion and prudence. Medical treatment and pastoral counseling remain the customary approach to healing.

hearsay

PRONUNCIATION: (*heer'·say*)

A reported statement or deed of another. If there is no confirming evidence of some kind, hearsay is considered useless in civil and criminal law. In a Christian setting, it is—at best—close to immoral to pay much attention to hearsay.

heaven

PRONUNCIATION: (*hev'·en*)

Paradise, the final state of reward and happiness of those saved by God through Christ, the just. See BEATIFIC VISION.

heavens

PRONUNCIATION: (*hev'·enz*)

A term found frequently in Scripture and thus in liturgy. It refers to the sky, the stars, and the heavenly bodies.

Hebrews

PRONUNCIATION: (*hee'·brewz*)

The people who formed the tribes of Israel and later the kingdoms of Israel and Judah. Their exact roots are uncertain, but they are revealed to us as God's chosen race. Hebrew is still used in Jewish worship and study. Although it had not been spoken among Jewish people since several centuries before Christ, it is now the official spoken language in Israel.

hedonism

PRONUNCIATION: (*hee'·dun·izm*)

A way of life that can be traced to ancient Greece, but also exists now. It is a kind of philosophy that sees the greatest happiness in seeking pleasure and avoiding pain.

hell

PRONUNCIATION: (*hell*)

The state of eternal punishment for those condemned because of sin. The greatest punishment of hell is believed to be the opposite of being with God in heaven, that is, being without God forever. One chooses hell by choosing against God.

heresy

PRONUNCIATION: (*hair'·ess·ee*)

A teaching opposed to the established teaching of the church. Heretics (those who embrace heresy) have often been devout, sincere people who went overboard in trying to understand one part of the Faith. Many were saintly people who actually made big contributions to the church.

hermeneutics

PRONUNCIATION: (her·muh·new'·tiks)

The study of the meaning of things found in Scripture. This is different from EXEGESIS. In practice the two often go hand in hand.

hierarchy

PRONUNCIATION: (hy'·ur'·ar·kee)

Those leaders of the church who belong to its officially established sacramental leadership: bishops, cardinals, the pope, etc.

holocaust

PRONUNCIATION: (holl'·uh'·kost)

In Scriptures, a highly destructive fire or other widespread destruction. In more recent time, holocaust refers to the attempt to destroy the Jewish people during World War II.

holy

PRONUNCIATION: (ho'·lee)

In normal use, godly, saintly, very religious. There are two other important meanings of the word if you trace its origins. One is "healthy." A holy person is one of true health. The other is "whole." Sinners are broken, fragmented; saints are whole. Holy also refers to special places and objects connected with religion.

holy days

PRONUNCIATION: (ho'·lee·dayz')

Special liturgical feasts such as the Feast of the Immaculate Conception. When the faithful are obliged to attend mass on such days, these days are known as holy days of obligation.

holy orders
PRONUNCIATION: *(ho'·lee·or'·derz)*
The SACRAMENT by which one becomes a member of the Catholic clergy—deacon, priest, or bishop. Formerly there were more orders, but they are now not strictly of the clergy.

Holy Spirit
PRONUNCIATION: *(ho'·lee·speer'·it)*
The third person of the Trinity. God's life dwelling in us now.

Holy Trinity
PRONUNCIATION: *(ho'·lee·trin'·it·ee)*
A vast, difficult mystery that is central to the Faith. It is a revelation to us by God of God's own nature. Three distinct persons—Father, Son, and Holy Spirit—are in one God. Attempts to explain further can lead to great confusion, even HERESY.

holy water
PRONUNCIATION: *(ho'·lee·wah'·ter)*
Blessed water used when entering church, in blessing the congregation, and in other liturgical actions. Among other things, it recalls our BAPTISM.

homily
PRONUNCIATION: *(hom·ill·ee)*
Preaching of the Word of God during eucharistic or other celebrations. A homily is a reflection and ex-

planation of the Scripture that is read during the celebration. The homily often has application for the present. A *sermon* is preaching that is not necessarily linked to the day's Scripture. The homily is the ordinary approach now.

hope

PRONUNCIATION: (*hope*)

A THEOLOGICAL VIRTURE. The virtue by which we trust in the promise of God, salvation, and eternal happiness for those who do God's will.

human rights

PRONUNCIATION: (*hew'·mun·rytes*)

Those rights that every person has. The right to human dignity as a creature of God. These include the right to reasonable food, clothing, shelter, health care, political freedom, useful employment, financial security, and just government. All recent popes have spoken and written brilliantly about human rights. One of the best was Pope John XXIII in the encyclical *Pacem in Terris* (*Peace on Earth*). Vatican II taught about human rights in *Gaudium et Spes* (*The Pastoral Constitution on the Church in the Modern World*).

humility

PRONUNCIATION: (*hew·mill·it·ee*)

A VIRTUE that is the opposite of PRIDE. All Christians should strive for humility. This does not mean that they should think themselves inferior, but they should recognize their dependence on God. Saint Theresa described humility simply as "truth."

I

icon

PRONUNCIATION: (eye·con)
From the Eastern tradition of the church, a two-dimensional image of Christ, Mary, or a saint.

idolatry

PRONUNCIATION: (eye·doll'·at·ree)
Worship of false gods. The Hebrew people took part in pagan rites involving Baal, the god of fertility. Ancient Greeks and Romans had many gods. Often, when we pay too much attention to wealth, power, comfort, and certain forms of enjoyment, we are guilty of a kind of idolatry. That doesn't mean that we are not to enjoy ourselves. We simply have to put first things first.

Immaculate Conception

PRONUNCIATION:
(im·mack'·yew·let·kun·sep'·shun)
A formal teaching of the church states that Mary was always free from ORIGINAL SIN. The term does not refer to the conception of Jesus by a virgin.

Immanuel

See EMMANUEL

immutable

PRONUNCIATION: (im·mew'·tuh·ble)
Unchangeable. There are a few things in our lives

that could be described in this way, but God is called immutable. God is, was, and shall be.

impediment

PRONUNCIATION: (im·ped'·uh·munt)
Something that stands in the way of the reception of a sacrament. For instance, a Catholic cannot marry a close blood relative; a married man cannot become a priest without a DISPENSATION.

incarnation

PRONUNCIATION: (in·kar·nay'·shun)
Literally, "something becoming flesh." In becoming human in the person of Jesus, God was incarnated—became one of us.

incense

PRONUNCIATION: (in'·sense)
From ancient times, people burned incense as a sign of respect for a higher power (god, ruler, etc.). On certain special occasions incense is used during the mass. On those occasions, the altar, the gifts of bread, wine, and our offerings, those gathered in prayer are incensed as a symbol of the church's offering all to God.

incomprehensible

PRONUNCIATION: (in'·kom·pree·hen'·sih·bull)
Not capable of being grasped or understood. This is an important word to us because it is a basic teaching of Christianity that God is incomprehensible. We can know a lot about God through revelation and spiritual experience; however, no finite, mortal

person can ever fully know the great, eternal God, at least not in this life.

indifferentism
PRONUNCIATION: (in·diff'·rent·izm)
A direction of religious belief that holds all religions to be about equal.

indulgence
PRONUNCIATION: (in·dull'·gentz)
Removing all or part of the temporal punishment of sin as a reward for prayer or good works. The church teaches that although sin is forgiven and eternal punishment removed through PENANCE or perfect contrition, temporal punishment remains. (See PURGATORY.)

inerrancy
PRONUNCIATION: (in·air'·un·see)
Usually used regarding Scripture. There are scientific and factual "errors" in the Bible if it is read literally. That is why skilled interpretation through the church is necessary. A general principle is that the Bible is free from error only in the language used by the author in the sense the author intended.

infallibility
PRONUNCIATION: (in·fahl'·ih·bill'·it·ee)
Catholics believe that grace preserves the teachings of the church from error when the church formally states that something must be believed. All truths that God has revealed to the church through Christ are protected from error. The preservation of the

church from error in its teachings on faith and morals is because of the protection of the Holy Spirit. A teaching is infallible only when formally proclaimed infallible by the pope, or by the bishops teaching in union with the pope.

infinite

PRONUNCIATION: (in'·fin·it)
Without limit or measure of any kind.

inspired

PRONUNCIATION: (in·spyrd')
The word implies activity of the Holy Spirit "breathed in." Usually used regarding Scripture. Prompted by God to speak or write. The authors communicated God's message through their own human ways of expression.

institution narrative

PRONUNCIATION:
(in'·stih·too·shun·nar'·uh·tiv)
When we recall in the mass the words and actions of Christ at the LAST SUPPER when he instituted the EUCHARIST.

intercessions

PRONUNCIATION: (in·tur·sesh'·unz)
Within the mass, it is a series of prayers for the church, the world, the pope, clergy and laity, and those who have died. In general, an intercession is any prayer calling to mind our needs or the needs of others.

70

general intercessions

PRONUNCIATION: (jen·er·ul·in·tur·sesh·unz)

A prayer in the mass in which we consider and pray for the needs of humanity. In this prayer we recall the church and its needs, the needs of governments and civil authorities, the particular needs of those we love and care for, and for the salvation and peace of the world. The priest celebrant usually invites us to pray while another minister announces the petitions and all those gathered respond (often with a phrase like "Lord, hear our prayer" or "Lord, grant us what we ask").

J

Jehovah

PRONUNCIATION: (jih·hoe'·vah)

A name of God now commonly used by English-speaking Protestants. It is compounded from two Hebrew words: *JHVH* or ADONAI. Christian soldiers misread the two forms as one, subsequently, the erroneous Jehovah. See YAHWEH.

Jerusalem

PRONUNCIATION: (jer·ew'·suh·lem)

The house of God, the city of God, the Holy City. The place where the temple was during Jesus' lifetime.

Jesuit

PRONUNCIATION: (jes'·yew·it)

A term for a member of the Society of Jesus, founded by Saint Ignatius Loyola. The Jesuit tradition stresses discipline, independence, and great loyalty to the pope. Historically, there was a military flavor. We know Jesuits best as teachers and scholars, but their number has always included great missioners, preachers, and pastors.

Jesus

PRONUNCIATION: (jee'·zus)

The name given to our Savior, born of Mary. It means "Yahweh saves."

Judeo-Christian tradition

PRONUNCIATION:
(jew·day'·oh·kris'·chun·tra·dish·un)

Our roots are found in the life and in the worship of the Hebrew people. Early Christianity grew out of Judaism. Therefore, our tradition is called Judeo-Christian.

judgment

PRONUNCIATION: (judge'·munt)

We teach that God will judge each person at death and all people in a general judgment. Eternal reward or punishment will depend on such judgment. This is the privilege of God alone. We should never judge the moral character of others.

justice

PRONUNCIATION: (jus'·tiss)

Generally means giving each person what is due to

that person. It means observing and protecting individual rights as well as doing the things we are supposed to do to serve people and the community. It is a major VIRTUE. Where justice is absent, so is Christianity.

justification

PRONUNCIATION: *(jus'·tih·fih·kay·shun)*

Sinful humanity being made just by God. God freely brings humanity into proper relationship with God by giving us a share in the divine nature. (See HOLY SPIRIT.)

just war

PRONUNCIATION: *(just·war)*

Traditionally, we have taught that war can be just if our motives are right and we fight honorably. This would be particularly true in defending one's own country. However, history indicates that few wars have been truly just and that any modern war may be immoral because of its horrible consequences. A Catholic may choose to oppose all war and refuse to take part in war.

K

kenosis

PRONUNCIATION: *(key·no'·sis)*

A Greek word meaning "emptying out." Christ emptied himself for us through his Passion and death. Christians are called to empty themselves of

73

sin, of selfish desires, and even of some good things, in order to move toward perfection.

kerygma

PRONUNCIATION: (*ker·ig'·ma*)

A term popular in religious education in recent years. It comes from the Greek word *keryx*, meaning "messenger." The kerygma is the body of the message of God through Christ, the GOOD NEWS of salvation.

kingdom of God

PRONUNCIATION: (*king·dum·uv·gahd*)

The term can refer to heaven, to the CHURCH, or to the past, present, and future reign of God. The sense of the past, present, and future reign of God is the most common now. God's reign depends on our being God's subjects. Our task is to extend God's reign over all the earth until the final coming of the eternal kingdom.

koinonia

PRONUNCIATION: (*koyn·own'·ee·uh*)

A Greek term for "fellowship." Used in a special sense among Christians, it refers to brotherhood in love extended to ordinary living, especially within the Christian community.

Koran

PRONUNCIATION: (*ko·ran*)

The holy book of the Muslims. It contains the revelations of God to Mohammed, and it is the basis of the religion of Islam.

kosher

PRONUNCIATION: (ko·shur)
Sanctioned by Jewish law; especially, ritually blessed for use by Jewish people.

Kyrie Eleison

PRONUNCIATION: (koo·roo·yay·ay·lay·ee·zown)
"Lord, have mercy."

Kyrios

See LORD.

L

laity

PRONUNCIATION: (lay·it·ee)
The people of the church who are not clergy. Members of religious communities are normally considered different from the laity. However, unless members of a religious community are ordained, they are, strictly speaking, *lay religious.*

lamb

PRONUNCIATION: (lam)
In the church, a symbol for Christ, the innocent Lamb who was slain in sacrifice for our sin.

Last Supper

PRONUNCIATION: (last·supp·ur)
The meal shared by Jesus and his closest followers on the eve of his PASSION. It was during this meal that the EUCHARIST was instituted.

law

PRONUNCIATION: (law)

A solemnly enacted or decreed rule of conduct. The Old Testament use of the term refers to the LAW OF MOSES and the rules derived from that. We also refer to the law of Christ—love. There are several kinds of laws in the church, not all equally binding and many subject to change.

Law of Moses

PRONUNCIATION: (law·uv·mo'·zis)

A term for the first five books of the Old Testament, known as the Pentateuch. At one time, Moses was thought to be its author. In the Jewish tradition this Law is contained in the TORAH.

lectern

PRONUNCIATION: (lek'·turn)

The place where the scriptures are read. Reading the scriptures from the lectern is called proclaiming the scriptures.

lectionary

PRONUNCIATION: (lek'·shun·ary)

The book that contains all of the readings from the scriptures for use in the celebration of the LITURGY.

lector

PRONUNCIATION: (lek'·tur)

Means "reader." One who reads sacred SCRIPTURE during liturgy. This is a specific ministry which can be held or exercised by laymen and laywomen or by those preparing for the priesthood who receive a commission to perform this service.

Lent

PRONUNCIATION: *(lent)*
The forty-day preparation for the celebration of Easter. Lent is a time of PENANCE in order to get us ready to recall the Passion of Jesus, his death, and his Resurrection.

limbo

PRONUNCIATION: *(lim'·bow)*
It was believed that unbaptized infants who died spent eternity in a state of being called limbo. The belief is no longer common. It is currently held that God does not punish the innocent, including those who have not had formal BAPTISM.

liturgical year

PRONUNCIATION: *(lit·ur'·gee·kal·yeer)*
The calendar of feasts and seasons on which our daily worship is based. It celebrates the principal mysteries of the Faith, honors certain persons, and recalls important events in the history of salvation.

liturgy

PRONUNCIATION: *(lit'·ur·gee)*
The official public worship of the church. It includes the MASS, the SACRAMENTS, the DIVINE OFFICE, and the SACRAMENTALS. It is distinguished from "popular devotions" such as *novenas*, but such devotions are not discouraged when used appropriately.

Liturgy of the Word

PRONUNCIATION: *(lit·ur·gee·uv·thuh·wurd)*

The early part of the mass in which Scripture is read and reflected upon. The Liturgy of the Word also includes the HOMILY and the PRAYER OF THE FAITHFUL. On Sundays there are three readings: an Old Testament selection, a New Testament selection from the Epistles, and a Reading from the New Testament Gospels.

Living Bread

PRONUNCIATION: *(liv·ing·bred)*

A reference to the EUCHARIST. See BREAD OF LIFE.

Lord

PRONUNCIATION: *(lord)*

In general terms, a *lord* is a person of great power. In religious terms, the Lord is God, the ruler of all persons and all things.

M

Maccabees

PRONUNCIATION: *(mack'·ah·beez)*

A nickname for a family that led a revolt by the Jews against the Seleucids in 165 B.C. *Maccabees* means "hammer." The name also applies to two Old Testament books not accepted by all Christians as authentic.

magisterium

PRONUNCIATION: (*mah·jus·ter'·ee·um*)

The teaching authority of the CHURCH as carried out by the HIERARCHY. However, particularly since Vatican II, it has been held that anyone can contribute to the teaching of the church, as long as it is done through established organization. In other words, because of their special knowledge, a physician, a scientist, a lawyer, or a historian may contribute to Catholic teaching.

Magnificat

PRONUNCIATION: (*mag·nif'·ee·kat*)

The canticle of the Blessed Virgin sung or recited during evening prayer. The term comes from the word *magnify*. "My soul magnifies the Lord . . ."

man, mankind, humanity

PRONUNCIATION:
(*man·man·kynd·hew·man·uh·tee*)

These words are used in Scripture and liturgy of the church to include all persons.

marks of the church

PRONUNCIATION: (*marks·uv·thuh·churtch*)

Traditional signs of what one would expect to find in the true CHURCH of Christ. It would be one, holy, CATHOLIC, and APOSTOLIC. (See APOSTOLIC SUCCESSION.)

martyr

PRONUNCIATION: (*mar·tur*)

One who gives her or his life for the Faith. Many

early Christians and later saints were martyrs. There are also martyrs in modern times.

mass

PRONUNCIATION: (mass)

The LITURGY of the EUCHARIST, main act of Catholic worship. The term comes from the old form of dismissal from worship: "Ite missa est." Missa, from which the word mass derives, means "sent."

master

PRONUNCIATION: (mass'·tur)

One having authority, control, or considerable knowledge or skill. In the New Testament, sometimes the term is used as a form of address for Jesus. Sometimes Jesus himself uses the term. The general sense is "rabbi" or "teacher."

matrimony (marriage)

PRONUNCIATION: (mat·rih'·mo·nee)

The SACRAMENT in which a man and woman are joined for life in a special way before God. So solemn and serious is this relationship that it is used as an image of Christ's relationship to the church and Yahweh's to Israel.

mediator

PRONUNCIATION: (mee'·dee·ay·tor)

Jesus is our Mediator with the Father most especially in the liturgy. An old liturgical expression says that we receive from the Father through the Son and return to the Father through the Son in the

Spirit. Jesus, God in flesh, is our obvious close link to God unseen.

meditation

PRONUNCIATION: (meh·dih·tay·shun)

Thinking and reflecting about God and about our relationship to God, often following spiritual reading. It is intended to lead to MENTAL PRAYER and is considered essential to real spiritual growth.

menorah

PRONUNCIATION: (men·oh·rah)

A candelabra. In the Old Testament Book of Exodus (25:31–40), the candlestick is described as being made of pure gold, having seven branches, and holding lamps that were kept constantly burning in the temple.

mental prayer

PRONUNCIATION: (men·tul·prayr)

Not simply silent prayer, but a silent lifting of the mind and heart to God in prayer that may go beyond words.

mercy

PRONUNCIATION: (mur·see)

A virtue through which one serves the poor or suffering simply because they are poor and suffering. Compassion. Applied CHARITY. Also, mercy can be referred to in judgment and punishment. We hope God will judge us with mercy. "Justice must be tempered with mercy."

Messiah

PRONUNCIATION: *(mess·i'·uh)*

Literally, "anointed one," which is also the meaning of the word CHRIST. The Messiah was the leader, promised by God, who was looked for by the Jews in the Old Testament. We believe Jesus was the Messiah.

messianic people

PRONUNCIATION: *(mess·ee·an·ik·pee·pul)*

The people of God carrying on the saving mission of Christ in union with him.

mezuzah

PRONUNCIATION: *(miss·oo'·zuh)*

The name given to a small container that holds a parchment on which the texts of Deuteronomy 6:4–9 and 11:13–21 have been inscribed. This container is meant to be affixed to the door post of a house. The verses from Scripture express a profession of faith in God and the command to love God.

Midrash

PRONUNCIATION: *(mid'·rash)*

Stories handed down and worked into (Old Testament) Scripture to tell about persons or events. These stories were largely fictional, but they were not meant to be misleading. Their purpose was to make a point, to add meaning. The Hebrews used many such devices in their teaching.

ministers of communions

PRONUNCIATION:

(*min'·iss·turz·uv·ko·mewn'·yunz*)

Those who assist in the distribution of communions. Deacons, priests and bishops are the ordinary ministers of communions. Special Ministers of communion are lay persons designated to assist in the distribution of communion when there is pastoral need. Special Ministers used to be called Extraordinary Ministers.

ministry

PRONUNCIATION: (*min'·iss·tree*)

Literally, "serving another or others." In the church there are many ministries, not all of which involve priests. Our appreciation of that concept is growing, but it is an old notion, rooted in the teachings of Saint Paul.

miracle

PRONUNCIATION: (*mir'·uh·kul*)

An event attributed to supernatural power and taken as a sign of God's presence and activity. It would involve HEALING or a phenomenon such as a dramatic change in the way things normally happen that would be beyond understanding except in terms of God's power.

mission

PRONUNCIATION: (*mish'·shun'*)

A task for which one is sent. A place in which missionary activity is carried out. Foreign missions are the church's work among non-Christians in distant lands. Home missions are those in our own country in areas where the church is not well established.

missionary
PRONUNCIATION: (miss·shun'·air·ee)
Work in a MISSION. More commonly, one who works in a mission. A missionary may be male or female, priest, religious, or lay person. Sometimes the term *missioner* is used instead.

monastery
PRONUNCIATION: (mahn'·uh'·stair·ee)
A place where MONKS live and work. There is usually a large chapel, a library, a residence, and often a farm or school. Some monasteries are more closed to the outside world than others. Some MONKS leave monasteries for various periods to perform the work of the church.

monk
PRONUNCIATION: (munk)
One who strives for spiritual perfection in a religious community. Generally, a monk works and prays within the MONASTERY, but some leave at times to minister to others in teaching, parish work, etc. See CONTEMPLATION.

monotheism
PRONUNCIATION: (mah'·no'·thee·izm)
Belief in one God.

morality

PRONUNCIATION: (mor·al'·it·ee)

Individual and social conduct, in relation to the law and will of God.

mortal

PRONUNCIATION: (mor·tul)

Deadly. That which works against the power of GRACE in our lives. That we are mortal often means that we are cut off in some way from God and humankind. See MORTAL SIN.

mortal sin

PRONUNCIATION: (mor·tul·sin)

Means sin that is deadly, sin serious enough to bring eternal punishment. Modern thought favors viewing this kind of sin more as a state of rejecting or deliberately ignoring God than as a single evil act. To be defined as mortal sin, such sin as an act would have to include grave wrong, full knowledge of the evil involved, and free consent of the will. This is possible, but probably not as common as was once thought.

mortification

PRONUNCIATION: (mor·tih·fih·kay·shun)

Bringing the body and its passions under control by practices of penance. Fasting, silence, self-denial, simple or crude clothing, little sleep, and hard labor are among the practices. Mortification is an old notion with a sound basis in tradition. We must die to ourselves to find real life in God.

Mother of God

PRONUNCIATION: (muth·ur·uv·gahd)

A name for the Blessed Virgin Mary. As mother of Jesus, who was God in the flesh, she became in a real sense, Mother of God. Of course, God existed always.

Mysteries of the Rosary

PRONUNCIATION:
(miss'·ter·eez·uv·thuh·row·zar·ee)

There are fifteen events in the lives of Jesus and Mary that we meditate on, five at a time, when praying the Rosary.

The Joyful Mysteries: (1) the Annunciation, (2) the Visitation, (3) the Nativity of Jesus, (4) the Presentation of Jesus at the Temple, and (5) the Finding of Jesus in the Temple.

The Sorrowful Mysteries: (1) the Agony in the Garden, (2) the Scourging at the Pillar, (3) the Crowning with Thorns, (4) the Carrying of the Cross, and (5) the Crucifixion.

The Glorious Mysteries: (1) the Resurrection, (2) the Ascension, (3) Pentecost, (4) the Assumption of Mary, and (5) the Coronation of Mary in Heaven.

mystery

PRONUNCIATION: (miss'·ter·ee)

A truth we can know something about but will never be able to fully understand or explain.

mystical body

See BODY OF CHRIST.

myth

PRONUNCIATION: *(mith)*

A story that teaches a deep truth that would be hard to express otherwise. There are wild legends and stories called myths; but actual myth teaches truth. Myth is found in Scripture and echoes in the liturgy where it is told through RITUAL. Myth aids in understanding reality.

N

name

PRONUNCIATION: *(naym)*

A word or words by which a person or thing is regularly known. As a rule, we take names of saints at baptism and confirmation. A Jewish name tells something about a person and that person's family. The Holy Name is that of Jesus. "God calls each man by his own name."

novena

PRONUNCIATION: *(no·vee'·nuh)*

A devotion lasting nine days. Novenas were popular recently as devotions to the Blessed Mother or to one of the saints. They are less common now, but still a rich source of prayer.

novitiate

PRONUNCIATION: *(no·vish'·ee·ut)*

A spiritual training period and time of testing for a man or woman entering a religious order or community. It usually lasts one year and is required by church law. If a novice completes this period successfully, she or he usually takes temporary vows to try the life further and finally makes solemn profession or takes lifetime vows.

nun

PRONUNCIATION: (*nun*)

A woman who takes vows as a member of a religious order or community. She seeks to live the spiritual life while serving the church by teaching, nursing, or other ministry.

nuncio

See APOSTOLIC DELEGATE.

O

obedience

See POVERTY, CHASTITY, OBEDIENCE.

occasion of sin

PRONUNCIATION: (*oh·kay·zhun·uv·sin*)

A person, place, or thing that can or does lead us to sin. Whenever possible, occasions of sin are to be avoided. Sometimes we must approach them for a serious reason, such as the good of another person, and in such cases, we do the best we can to avoid sin.

Offertory

PRONUNCIATION: (*off'·ur'·tor·ee*)

The time during the mass when the gifts are brought to the altar and prepared for the Sacrifice.

oil

PRONUNCIATION: (oyl)

There is rich symbolism connected with the use of oil in religion. In Old Testament times and even outside the Hebrew tradition oil was used to mark a person or thing as holy or sacred. Kings were anointed. *Christ* means "the anointed one." Oil was also a medicinal or healing sign, giving double symbolism to our ANOINTING OF THE SICK. Oil is also a sign of joy and festivity, used in baptism, confirmation, and holy orders.

Oplatek

PRONUNCIATION: (oh·plah'·tek)

A singularly beautiful custom among Polish Catholics at Christmas time. At the *Wigilia* (vigil at which the crib is blessed), the people break bread with one another. The bread is much like that found in hosts. As they do this, they forgive each other for all the offenses of the past year. This practice is also conducted outside the *Wigilia*.

ordinary

PRONUNCIATION: (or'·dih·nair·ee)

Refers to the person usually having authority in the church in a given place. Usually it refers to a bishop. A bishop is often called the *local ordinary*.

ordinary means

PRONUNCIATION: (or·dih·nair·ee·meenz)

That which one is expected to make use of in a given situation. For example, when one is sick, one should seek good health care, receive treatment, take medicine, etc. We are not bound to use *extraordinary means* to preserve health or even life. Extraordinary means are things that are very expensive, painful, unusual, and offer little or no hope of true recovery.

ordinary time

PRONUNCIATION: (or·dih·nair·ee·tyme)
Times in the CHURCH YEAR, outside Lent, Christmas, and other special seasons.

ordination

PRONUNCIATION: (or·dih·nay'·shun)
Placing in order. In the church, the term refers to solemn ceremonies in which one becomes a priest, bishop, or deacon. Thus, he becomes ordained; he receives a share in the sacrament of HOLY ORDERS, which is enjoyed fully only by bishops.

Ordo

PRONUNCIATION: (or·doe)
A book that lists the seasons and feasts of the LITURGICAL YEAR. It tells the proper mass and DIVINE OFFICE for each day. It is the order of our daily worship. There is some variation depending on geography.

original sin

PRONUNCIATION: (*oh·ridge·in·ul·sin*)
We are born into a world of sin, and the world of sin is within us. From this, only God can save us,

and God does so through Christ. The church teaches that sin is acquired through generation, in a sense inherited from the first of humankind. Original Sin is removed by BAPTISM.

Orthodox Jew

PRONUNCIATION: (or'·tho'·dox·jew)

In accordance with the strictest of the three major divisions of Judaism, Orthodox Jews follow the Jewish rules and all the old rites, traditions, ceremonies, and customs. They wear *yarmulkes* (skull caps), and they take the Bible literally and follow it as best they can. Orthodox Jews live strictly by the laws set forth in the TORAH and Talmud.

Orthodoxy

PRONUNCIATION: (or'·tho·dox'·ee)

The word has two meanings. The first refers to correct, traditional beliefs. The second refers to Eastern Churches that are quite Catholic in their beliefs and worship but do not recognize the pope as universal leader. We have been close to them since Vatican II. Eastern Rite churches that do recognize the pope are known as *Uniate*.

P

pagan religions

PRONUNCIATION: (*pay·gun·ree·lidge·uns*)

Generally, religions outside the JUDEO-CHRISTIAN TRADITION.

palm

PRONUNCIATION: (*pahlm*)

The disciples bore palms when Jesus entered Jerusalem shortly before his PASSION. Traditionally, the palm is a sign of martyrdom. In the Hebrew tradition, palms were used to decorate the temple.

Palm Sunday

PRONUNCIATION: (*pahlm'·sun·day*)

The Sunday before Easter. The liturgy of this day recalls the entrance of Jesus into Jerusalem before his PASSION. On that day, the disciples bore palms.

pantheism

PRONUNCIATION: (*pan·thee·izm*)

Roughly, the idea that everything is divine. Failure to make a distinction between the creator and what has been created.

parables

PRONUNCIATION: (*pahr'·uh·bulz*)

The stories Jesus used to teach religious truths to ordinary people. He taught in terms of farming, housekeeping, conduct of business—things most people would understand easily.

parish

PRONUNCIATION: (*pahr'·ish*)

A small local section of the church usually headed by a pastor who is a priest or by a pastoral team often consisting of priests, religious, and sometimes lay persons.

Paschal Mystery

PRONUNCIATION: (pass'·kul·miss'·ter·ee)

The Passion, death, Resurrection, and Ascension of Jesus. This is the central event in Christianity, on which everything else is based. It is the essence of our salvation by God through God's Son.

Passion

PRONUNCIATION: (pash'·un)

The suffering of Jesus after his betrayal by Judas Iscariot. He was mistreated, subjected to false trials, scourged, crowned with thorns, and crucified. His death on the cross following this suffering is seen as his atonement for the sins of all of us.

Passover

PRONUNCIATION: (pass'·ovur)

The celebration by the Jewish people of their deliverance from Egypt, through which God freed them from slavery (Exodus 4–15).

peace

PRONUNCIATION: (pees)

We all know the word *peace*, but it has special depth in Christianity. It is something Christ brought as the Prince of Peace. We wish each other peace during the mass. This wish should never be halfhearted or mechanical. It means we forgive everyone and wish them the deep joy of a peaceful mind and heart in a world that seems often to believe that peace is impossible. In this sense, peace means much more than the absence of war.

penance

PRONUNCIATION: (pen'·unse)

The sacrament through which people are reconciled to each other and to God, and by which their sins are forgiven. It is a SACRAMENT of the people (in that it begins and ends with them), by the people (in that they co-celebrate it with the priest), and for the people (in that it is a gift of God, always available, to help them on their way to unity with God). See also DOING PENANCE.

penitential rite

PRONUNCIATION: (pen'·uh·ten·shul·ryte)

Usually refers to the part of the mass in which all those present admit sinfulness and call upon God to show mercy on us.

Pentecost

PRONUNCIATION: (pen'·tuh'·kost)

The coming of the Holy Spirit to the close followers of Jesus after the Ascension. In a real sense, this was the beginning of the active church.

Pentecostal

PRONUNCIATION: (pen·tuh·kos'·tul)

The term refers to persons or sects that place great emphasis on the activity of the Holy Spirit. The Spirit's activity is surely present in daily life, but wisdom and restraint are needed to understand it and work with it. See DISCERNMENT.

People of God

PRONUNCIATION: *(pee·pull·uv·gahd)*
An ancient term revived during the 1960s to describe the community of believers. It grows from the description of the people of the Old Testament who followed Yahweh. Although God's covenant with them remains, we now use the term to refer to the followers of Christ—a priestly, kingly, prophetic people among whom no one is unimportant.

pharisaical scandal

PRONUNCIATION: *(fair·uh·say'·ee·kul·scan·dl)*
A person or a group getting upset, as the PHARISEES would, over a minor wrong or a mere legalistic matter.

Pharisees

PRONUNCIATION: *(fair'·uh·seez)*
A class of Jewish leaders during the time of Jesus. Originally they were pious and very respectful of law. They had great influence. However, their exaggerated piety and legalism turned into hypocrisy and burdened the people. Jesus criticized them severely many times.

philosophy

PRONUNCIATION: *(fil·oss'·uf·ee)*
A study in which we reflect on, criticize, and try to explain wisdom, being, experience, norms of conduct, all of life. The roots of philosophy are ancient, and it has changed greatly as science has de-

veloped. It is not tied to theology, but it can be an aid to theology at times. Its challenges to religion do not disprove religion, but call on theologians to study more deeply and offer better explanations.

polytheism

PRONUNCIATION: (*poll·ee·thee'·izm*)
Belief in many gods.

pontiff

PRONUNCIATION: (*pon'·tiff*)
He who has the highest place and greatest authority. The POPE is the pontiff of the Roman Catholic Church.

Pontius Pilate

PRONUNCIATION: (*pon'·chus·py'·lut*)
The Roman governor of Judea during the time that Jesus lived in the Holy Land.

pope

PRONUNCIATION: (*pohp*)
The visible head of the church. The bishop of Rome. The pope is elected by the CARDINALS. He is the chief pastor and teacher of the church. See INFALLIBILITY.

poverty, chastity, obedience

PRONUNCIATION:
(*pov'·ur·tee·chass'·tih·tee·oh'·bee'·dee·unse*)
The vows taken by nuns, brothers, and priests who become members of religious orders. Also known as the *Evangelical (Gospel) Counsels.* Persons in

vows promise to live in poverty, to sacrifice legitimate sexual pleasure in marriage, and to obey their superiors. This is done in imitation of Christ and is known as the state of perfection, or at least an excellent approach to it.

pragmatism
PRONUNCIATION: (prag'·muh·tizm)
An approach to life based on the idea that if a thing works it is good. Using pragmatism as the sole standard of worth is a very limited approach to living, and it is not consistent with Christianity.

prayer
PRONUNCIATION: (prayr)
The method by which the individual and the community attempt to speak to God. It can involve asking for things, being sorry for things, or simply praising and adoring God. Prayer is essential to Christian life and should be practiced in more than mechanical form.

Prayer of the Faithful
PRONUNCIATION: (prayr·uv·thuh·fayth'·full)
The prayer offered during the mass before the Offertory, when petitions are offered to God on behalf of those present and the whole church. Also known as the *bidding prayers*.

predestination
PRONUNCIATION: (pree'·des'·tin·ay·shun)
The idea that God chooses in advance how we will do God's work on earth and how we will be with

God. It is a legitimate Catholic belief. We should remember, though, that such a life would still be lived in freedom. We should avoid making assumptions about our own predestination.

preface

PRONUNCIATION: (preh'·fus)

In the *preface* the priest celebrant praises the Father and gives thanks to God for the work of salvation and the special reasons for giving thanks on this particular day. This prayer of gratitude is the first element in the EUCHARISTIC PRAYER. It is either said or sung by the celebrant of the mass.

preface dialogue

PRONUNCIATION: (preh'·fus·dy'·uh·log)

The introduction to the prayer of the mass called the PREFACE. It is a dialogue because the priest celebrant of the mass and the people each share in saying the words of this prayer. In the preface dialogue we are invited to join in prayer and thanksgiving to God to whom all praise and thanksgiving is due.

presbyter

PRONUNCIATION: (prez'·bit·ur)

A title given to early Christian clergy who in the structure of the church were above deacons but lower than bishops. The term *priest* was not used widely before the fourth century.

presumption

PRONUNCIATION: (pre·zump'·shun)

An attitude wherein we assume that God will forgive us and protect us no matter what we do. This kind of thinking is dangerous and contrary to traditional teaching. We cannot save ourselves. God will give us what we need to be saved. However, it is up to us to seek God's aid and to make use of it.

pride

PRONUNCIATION: (*pryd*)

An attitude, or an out-and-out sin, in which we take too much credit for our good lives or actions. A Christian should not seek equality with God. God should be given credit for the good things a Christian does. No one should consider himself or herself better than another person. If a person has skills, gifts, or a good life, and has tried hard to perfect these things, that person could not have succeeded without God.

Priest-Prophet-King

PRONUNCIATION: (*preest/prof'·it/king*)

The roles of Christ that we take on through baptism and confirmation. As priests, we praise and offer sacrifice to God, lead others to God, and pray for them. In our role as prophets, God speaks through us. As kings, we help to bring order to creation.

private revelation

PRONUNCIATION: (*pry'·vet·rev'·ul·ay'·shun*)

When God speaks to an individual this is private revelation. It differs from those truths God has revealed to the whole Church and which must be believed by everyone.

problem of evil

PRONUNCIATION: (prob·lum·uv·ee'·vil)

An ancient riddle. How can an all-good God create a world in which there is such evil as starvation, war, and disease? How can an all-loving God allow it? There is no flat answer except that God will triumph over evil and that, through God, good often comes out of evil. Certainly God does not will evil. One approach is to view evil as the absence of good. If good is lacking, it is often the fault of humanity.

profane

PRONUNCIATION: (pro·fayn')

A negative term meaning not sacred, not religious, impure, defiled. This can apply to places, things, practices, thoughts, and language.

profession of faith

PRONUNCIATION: (pro·fesh'·un·uv·fayth)

In the profession of faith or creed the people gathered for liturgy respond to the word of God as proclaimed in the scriptures. It is a way in which believers say "yes" to their belief in fundamental teachings of the church. The profession of faith is used on all Sundays and other solemn feast days of the church year.

prophet

PRONUNCIATION: (prof'·it)

A special person through whom God speaks in order to teach some aspect of God's will or something about humanity's relationship to God. There are various uses of the term, but a true prophet would be called by God, and, aided by God, would teach through her or his own person and personality.

providence

PRONUNCIATION: (prov'·ih·dense)

Loving care for others before and while they need it. Divine Providence is God's loving care for us.

prudence

PRONUNCIATION: (prew'·dense)

A virtue by which a Christian makes the best choice of action or conduct in terms of his or her relationship to God as he or she understands God. Prudence is one of the CARDINAL VIRTUES.

psalm

PRONUNCIATION: (sahlm)

A song whose poetic form is found in the Old Testament. The psalms recount Salvation History, but they also cover a wide range of religious sentiment from penitence to praise of God. Psalms are sublime prayers, found in the Divine Office and throughout liturgy.

purgatory

PRONUNCIATION: (purr'·gah·tor·ee)

A name for a state of purification that we believe some people must pass through between life on earth and life in heaven.

purity

PRONUNCIATION: (*pure'·it·ee*)

A necessary but frequently misunderstood Christian VIRTUE. It means freedom from misuse of sex. It also means that acts or thoughts that could lead us to misuse of sex are to be avoided or controlled. It means a general spiritual cleanness, free from extreme concern with the flesh. However, purity alone does not make a person holy. Sins such as adultery are grave, but no more grave than many offenses that have nothing to do with sex.

R

rash judgment

PRONUNCIATION: (*rash·judge·munt*)

Making a judgment as to the right or wrong of an action without full knowledge and consideration of all the facts involved. If we presume a person is a sinner because of some little remark or action, we are judging rashly. See JUDGMENT.

Real Presence

PRONUNCIATION: (*reel'·prez'·uns*)

The doctrine taught by the church that the Body and Blood of Christ are sacrificed during the mass and fed to the faithful under the appearances of bread and wine. The mass is a commemoration of the LAST SUPPER. A Catholic must hold that Christ is truly present in the Eucharist. There are various ways of understanding the idea of Christ's presence. The Body is the risen, glorified Body of the Lord.

reconciliation

PRONUNCIATION: (*rek·un·sill·ee·ay·shun*)
Coming back together with a person or people from whom one is alienated. In the church, this is the effect of the sacrament of PENANCE. After sin and REPENTANCE, one is rejoined with God and the people of God.

Redeemer

PRONUNCIATION: (*ree·dee'·mur*)
Jesus Christ, the Son of God, who by his death offers salvation from sin to all the world. REDEMPTION is the gift of God given us in Jesus' life, death, and new life.

Redemption

PRONUNCIATION: (*ree·demp'·shun*)
Buying back, purchasing back, freeing from pawn. Jesus redeemed us from sin and death at the price of his own blood.

Reformation

PRONUNCIATION: (*ref·or·may'·shun*)
The tearing apart of the community of Christians during the sixteenth century. After a long period of corruption and abuse in the church, Martin Luther and other leaders rebelled. This led to a number of sects known as *Protestant*. We now see some of these leaders as heroes and Protestants as separated brothers and sisters.

Reformed Jew

PRONUNCIATION: (*ree·formd·jew*)

A Reformed Jew believes that understanding the meaning of the TORAH is more important than obeying it word for word. He believes in changing traditions, and if necessary, removing them.

relic

PRONUNCIATION: (*rel'·ik*)

Any object intimately connected with the life of a saint. Every regular altar must contain a relic, and relics are venerated in special places, for example, certain shrines and the Roman catacombs. There have been many false or questionable relics. The church takes great care before approving anything as a relic. The word means "memento" or "souvenir."

religious

PRONUNCIATION: (*ree·lidge'·us*)

A man or woman who has taken vows as a member of a RELIGIOUS ORDER or community and who is dedicated to the service of the church.

religious order

PRONUNCIATION: (*ree·lidge·us·or·dur*)

A formally organized community of priests, brothers, or nuns. They live under vows of POVERTY, CHASTITY, and OBEDIENCE and serve the church in various ways, ranging from simple labor to scholarship.

repentance

PRONUNCIATION: (ree·pen'·tunse)

Being sorry for a sinful way of life and turning away from it.

reputation

PRONUNCIATION: (rep·yew·tay·shun)

Each person has a right to a good reputation. If a person's reputation is truly deserved, the right is absolute. If it is not quite true, the person is still entitled to her or his good name. However, it is not immoral to reveal some harmful information about a person if it is necessary for the common good. In general, the good of the community comes before the good of the individual, although that doesn't mean that individual rights are not sacred.

revelation

PRONUNCIATION: (rev·ul·ay'·shun)

Communication of a truth from God to us. This occurs primarily through sacred Scripture and closely related church tradition. Revelation also takes place in an ongoing way through Christian community life. The term is also used for special experiences in which individuals, through visions or other exceptional events, have learned from God. This is called PRIVATE REVELATION and must be viewed with caution.

rite

PRONUNCIATION: (ryte)

A ceremony such as the mass (the Eucharistic Rite) or the rite of confirmation. Rite can also mean a specific division of the church, for example, the Latin or Eastern (Oriental) Rites. There are a number of rites within the Eastern Church. Generally they are linked to national background.

rites of penance

PRONUNCIATION: (*rytes·uv·pen'·unse*)

Current church practice includes three rites for the sacrament of PENANCE: (1) individual confession and ABSOLUTION, (2) communal service with individual confession and absolution, and (3) communal celebration with GENERAL ABSOLUTION.

ritual

PRONUNCIATION: (*rit·chual*)

In a religious sense, repeated patterns of behavior in a solemn setting. Ritual provides common ground for belief and for action expressing belief. There are also magical and even insane rituals. In a religious context, ritual comes close to being necessary for living a full human life.

the rock

PRONUNCIATION: (*thuh·rahk*)

A reference to Saint Peter, the rock on which Jesus founded his church. Many dispute the Catholic interpretation and deny any such office as the papacy. We are safe in following the traditional interpretation and surely in believing Jesus gave his church a foundation "of rock." See POPE.

Roman Catholic

PRONUNCIATION: (row'·mun·kath'·uh·lick')

The full name of the church. It means we belong to the universal Church founded by Christ. The center of its government since early Christian times is Rome.

rosary

PRONUNCIATION: (row'·zar·ee)

A wreath of flowers (at one time it meant roses). In the church, it is a wreath of prayers (Hail Marys), a special devotion to Mary. See MYSTERIES.

S

Sabbath

PRONUNCIATION: (sab·uth)

The traditional Jewish day of worship and rest, normally Saturday. The Jewish Sabbath traditions are rich, but are not completely the same as those of the Christian Sunday. Confusion of the two has led to misunderstanding in past church practices.

sacrament

PRONUNCIATION: (sack'·ruh·munt)

An action of Christ in and through the church to aid Christian people at particular stages of life (for example, marriage) or in particular situations (sickness). There are seven, and only seven, sacraments: BAPTISM, CONFIRMATION, MATRIMONY, PENANCE, ANOINTING OF THE SICK, HOLY ORDERS, and the EUCHA-

RIST. Reference to anything else as a sacrament is either metaphorical or false.

sacramental

PRONUNCIATION: (sack'·ruh·men'·tul)
A blessed object, practice, or rite that is not directly involved in one of the seven sacraments, but which may aid us in our spiritual growth. An example is the ROSARY.

sacramental confession

PRONUNCIATION: (sack·ruh·men'·tul·kun·fesh'·un)
Sharing our sinfulness in a special way with a priest and God. Asking God's forgiveness and showing willingness to change. See CONFESSION OF DEVOTION, RITES OF PENANCE.

sacrament of penance

See PENANCE.

sacramentary

PRONUNCIATION: (sak'·ruh·men'·tuh·ree)
The book used by the celebrant of the mass. This book contains all the prayers needed for the celebration of the liturgy of the mass.

sacred

PRONUNCIATION: (say'·kred)
Set aside for worship. Holy, worthy of great devotion. In a religious sense, very special.

sacrifice

PRONUNCIATION: (*sack'·ruh·fyse*)

A solemn religious action in which something is offered to God. This is usually done by a priest representing the people. The Mass is the perfect sacrifice, offering Christ and us with him. Other religious sacrifices are pagan, except in the sense of personal sacrifice, that is, giving up something either as a form of penance or for the good of another.

sacrilege

PRONUNCIATION: (*sack'·ruh·lidge*)

A serious offense wherein one insults God or some sacred thing. Examples are deliberately ridiculing a consecrated host or receiving Communion when one is sure of being in a state of grave sin.

sacristan

PRONUNCIATION: (*sack'·ris·tun*)

A person who has the duty of caring for the altar, the sacristy, the vestments, and anything else used in worship.

saint

PRONUNCIATION: (*saynt*)

A person officially declared by the church to be in heaven. The term was also used for all members of the early Christian communities. We are all called to be saints. As one preacher put it, "You either are one or you should be."

salvation

PRONUNCIATION: (sal·vay·shun)

The goal of all believers: deliverance from sin, victory over evil. We believe this comes from God through Christ and leads to eternal happiness.

Salvation History

PRONUNCIATION: (sal·vay'·shun·hiss'·tree)

A term for the series of events through which God revealed God's general plan for saving us. Salvation History includes God's covenant with Abraham; the Exodus; the events in the history of Israel that told of God's presence; and the life, death, and Resurrection of Christ. It is a theology of history in which we see God forming God's People and remaining with them, in spite of their sins and failures, as they journey through time toward fulfillment when Christ comes again.

sanctifying

PRONUNCIATION: (sank'·tiff·eye·ing)

Making something or someone holy. Bestowing the grace of God. See BLESSING.

sanctuary

PRONUNCIATION: (sank·chew'·air·ee)

A very holy place. The place where the altar is placed in a Catholic church; the portion of a Jewish temple where worship is conducted.

sanctus

PRONUNCIATION: (sank'·tuss)

The Latin word "sanctus" means holy. This prayer

in the mass begins with the words "Holy, Holy, Holy Lord." "The Holy" or "The Sanctus" as it is more generally called is the response we make to the PREFACE and continues prayers of gratitude in praise of God.

Savior

PRONUNCIATION: (sayv'·yur)

A title given to Jesus. His name means "Yahweh saves."

scandal

PRONUNCIATION: (skan'·dul)

An action or situation that leads others to sin or disgraces an institution such as the church.

scandals in the church

PRONUNCIATION: (skan·dulz·in·thuh·churtch)

Throughout history there have been times when we have had evil popes, immoral bishops, as well as priests, monks, nuns, and Catholic rulers who have been insane, criminal, or both. We must acknowledge this. The miracle is that for all the human error and fault we find in church history, the church has stood strong for two thousand years. Whatever the situation, the church always tries and eventually succeeds in communicating the message of Christ—the GOOD NEWS of the Gospel.

schism

PRONUNCIATION: (shiz·um)

A split or division in the church such as one between the East and West. A *schismatic* is one who separates, at least for a time, from the official

111

church. Often, in spite of a separation, a great deal of traditional belief and practice is retained.

science and religion
PRONUNCIATION: (sy·ents·and·ree·lidge·un)
Two concepts often thought to be opposed to each other. Catholic teaching is that there can be no contradiction between science, the study of what God has made, and THEOLOGY, the study of God. If contradiction appears, experts in one or both fields must study more deeply.

Scripture
PRONUNCIATION: (skrip'·tchur)
The books of the Bible, which we believe contain the history of the religious experience of our people as well as containing divine truth revealed by God to man. It is a Christian term. Hebrew people did not use the word Scripture for the Old Testament.

seal of confession
PRONUNCIATION: (seel·uv·kon·fesh'·un)
A strict law, strictly observed, that requires a priest to refuse to tell anything he has learned in confession, even if he is threatened by law or violence. The seal also covers interpreters or any others who may hear something that is confessed. These things may not even be discussed with the penitent outside of the confession unless the penitent asks for and agrees to such discussion.

Second Coming
PRONUNCIATION: (sek'·und·kum'·ing)
The coming of Christ in glory at the future high

point of Salvation History. At that time the kingdom of God will be perfected, and God will be all in all. Also called the *Parousia*.

secrets

PRONUNCIATION: (seek'·retz)

There are many kinds of secrets, things we learn and are supposed to keep to ourselves. Generally it is immoral to tell a serious secret. In most cases, a secret may be revealed if the person who confided it agrees or if the common good requires a warning (about a criminal or a disease, for instance). However, most professional secrets, like the secrets covered under the SEAL OF CONFESSION, may never be divulged.

secular

PRONUNCIATION: (sek'·yew·lur)

Of the world, as opposed to SACRED. Since Christ's coming, we know that worldliness does not mean evil. Christians are called to help the secular be its best, not to paint it holy. Too much attention to the secular, however, can lead to *secularism*, which is usually a denial of religious values and meaning. Secular is also a term used to describe priests of a diocese because they live in the world, not in a monastery.

secular institute

PRONUNCIATION: (sek'·yew·lur·in'·stih·toot)

A community of lay persons observing POVERTY, CHASTITY, and OBEDIENCE under private vows. Normally, in addition to serving the church in various ways, members work at regular occupations while seeking the spiritual life.

see

PRONUNCIATION: (*see*)

A territory or jurisdiction in the church. The *holy see* is the universal governing office of the church. The *diocesan see* is that of the local bishop. The principal city in a diocese is often called the *see city*.

segregation

PRONUNCIATION: (*seg'·ruh·gay'·shun*)

Enforced or deliberately planned separation of groups of people. For instance, the keeping apart of black and white, male and female.

seminary

PRONUNCIATION: (*sem'·in·aree*)

A school devoted to educating and forming priests. A seminary may be at the high school, college, or graduate school level. Normally eight years of study is required after high school. Religious and lay persons now study in some seminaries to prepare themselves for Christian ministry other than the ordained priesthood.

separated brethren

PRONUNCIATION: (*sep'·uh·ray·tud·breth'·ren*)

A term for Christians who are not members of the Roman Catholic Church. Since Vatican II, we regard them as true Christians who are separated from us, but not enemies or even opponents.

Septuagint

PRONUNCIATION: (sep'·too·uh·jint)

A translation of (what we call) the Old Testament into Greek by Jewish scholars before the birth of Christ.

sepulcher

PRONUNCIATION: (sep'·ul·kur)

A tomb or place of burial above ground. Christ was placed in a sepulcher after he died on the cross.

sexuality

PRONUNCIATION: (sex·yew·al·it·ee)

The term does not apply merely to sex acts, but to a person's whole makeup as a man or woman. Relationship to all the people we deal with is affected by our sexuality, so there is a definite Christian reason for understanding it. Our sexuality is an important part of our spiritual life.

shalom

PRONUNCIATION: (sha·lowm')

A Jewish greeting now used often among Christians. It means "peace."

sign of peace

PRONUNCIATION: (syne·uv·pees)

Before we share the Eucharist in communion we are invited to share with one another. When we celebrate the peace of the Lord we express peace and love with one another, unity with the church, and all humanity.

simony

PRONUNCIATION: (sim'·uh·nee)

The buying or selling of sacred and religious offices and privileges. A grave crime in the church. Although this practice is rare now, it was common before the REFORMATION.

sin

PRONUNCIATION: (sin)

An act or omission that offends God because it shows lack of love for God or for people. Although actions or omissions can be sinful, serious sin is more probably a state in which we reject or neglect God and God's love.

sister

PRONUNCIATION: (sis'·tur)

A female sibling. In the church, we are all brothers and sisters, but the title "sister" is given to NUNS.

situation ethics

PRONUNCIATION: (sit·chew·ay'·shun·eth'·iks)

Attempts to determine whether actions are right or wrong based solely on circumstances and effects. This approach denies the existence of objective moral standards. Everything becomes relative. Catholic ethics considers circumstances and effects, but it holds that there are objective standards of right and wrong and that some things are wrong in and of themselves.

Son of man

PRONUNCIATION: (sun·uv·man)

A term Jesus used to refer to himself. It is also used in a wider, more mysterious sense and is found in Scripture often (eighty-two times in the Gospels). Jesus' choice of these words shows his willingness to fully partake in all that is human.

soul

PRONUNCIATION: (sowl)

The spiritual aspect of a human person; that which makes an individual more than animal; that which survives the death of the body. During a person's earthly life, body and soul are united. We teach that body and soul will be reunited at the general resurrection. Just how is a mystery of the Faith. For many theologians, the soul is the direct image of God in a person. In the Hebrew sense, the term means more the heart of the individual, the essence of what it means to be a person.

Spirit of Jesus

PRONUNCIATION: (speer'·it·uv·jeez'·us)

A reference to the Holy Spirit, true God and third person of the Trinity. This title comes from the fact that Christ promised—and kept his promise—to send the Spirit, which appeared at PENTECOST.

spirituality

PRONUNCIATION: (speer'·it·chew·al'·it·ee)

A process through which one strives to improve one's relationship with God. Spirituality involves a person's overall idea of God, as well as involving prayer, reflection, and the way in which love of God and of people is lived out in daily action.

spouse
PRONUNCIATION: (spows)
Partner by marriage—a husband or wife of a person. Someone who has made a commitment before God and the world to share life with another person.

Stations of the Cross
PRONUNCIATION: (stay·shunz·uv·thuh·kross)
Also known as the WAY OF THE CROSS. A devotion that focuses prayer and meditation on fourteen events in the Passion and death of Jesus. Many times a fifteenth station is added to celebrate the Resurrection.

stole
PRONUNCIATION: (stowl)
A vestment worn about the neck to signify church office. Priests, bishops and deacons wear the stole during liturgical functions. Deacons wear it across the left shoulder, crossed and fastened at the right side.

suffering servant
PRONUNCIATION: (suf'·ring·sir'·vunt)
A figure in prophecy (for example, Isaiah) who is innocent but suffers for others. This is seen as an Old Testament figure of the Christ or Messiah who was to come.

superstition

PRONUNCIATION: (*soup·ur·stish'·un*)

Belief that certain persons or things have powers
that we believe belong only to God. Examples
would be belief in fortunetelling or belief that a
certain ritual brings good luck (for example, carrying a rabbit's foot).

symbol

PRONUNCIATION: (*sim'·bul*)

Something concrete that stands for something else.
The cross, for instance, reminds us of the whole
mystery of Christ. Signs and symbols help us to express and to understand religious truth.

T

tabernacle

PRONUNCIATION: (*tab'·ur·nak·ul*)

The compartment in the church where the Blessed
Sacrament is kept. The word can mean any place
where a sacred thing is stored. As used in the Old
Testament, and once in the New Testament, it
means "tent." The Hebrew people lived in tents
while in the desert after escaping from Egypt. They
still celebrate a Feast of the Tabernacles.

Ten Commandments
See COMMANDMENTS

testament

PRONUNCIATION: (tes'·tuh·munt)

Means witness, evidence, creed, handing on of property (as in a will). The Bible is divided into the Old and New Testaments. These testaments are evidence of our claim to religious truth; they give witness to our belief; and they are sources of our creed that are handed on from days and people past.

theological virtues

PRONUNCIATION:
(the'·uh'·lah·gee·kul·vir'·chuz)

Faith, hope, and charity (love).

Faith: belief in God as we understand God.

Hope: being willing to "turn our lives over" to the care and concern of our loving God.

Charity: love of God, ourselves, and our neighbors.

See VIRTUE.

theology

PRONUNCIATION: (thee·ahl'·uh·gee)

A study that methodically seeks to learn and explain God's REVELATION. The study of God as we have come to understand God in human history. Theology attempts to explain what we believe.

third orders

PRONUNCIATION: (thurd·or·durz)

Groups of lay persons who pursue their regular lives while living in the spirit of a religious order, such as the FRANCISCANS or the DOMINICANS. They have rules, and they meet with the affiliated religious communities. BENEDICTINES have similar affiliates, called *oblates*.

tonsure

PRONUNCIATION: *(ton'·shur)*

Cutting the hair of a candidate for the priesthood as a mark of being set apart for the special service of Christ through the church. The practice has been discontinued, although some monastic communities still cut or shave some or all of a candidate's hair.

Torah

PRONUNCIATION: *(tow·rah)*

The Hebrew word for "instruction," "direction," or "law." Particularly used in the sense of the first five books of the Bible, often called the Pentateuch.

tradition

PRONUNCIATION: *(tra·dish'·un)*

Any teaching handed down from one generation to another. The holy teaching of the church. Also, a belief or practice that grows out of the long life of an institution. At one time we considered Scripture and tradition as sources of revelation in the church. Vatican II taught that Scripture and tradition are more like one interacting source.

Transfiguration

PRONUNCIATION: *(tranz·fig'·yew'·ray·shun)*

The glorification of Jesus before Peter, James, and John as related in the Gospels. Jesus was transfigured into heavenly beauty on a mountain. This is considered a sign of his divinity. The apostles were impressed greatly but they did not fully understand the meaning of the event. Some say it was a way of strengthening their faith in preparation for the time when they would see Jesus treated as a criminal, beaten, and executed.

triangle
PRONUNCIATION: *(try·angle)*
In Christianity, a symbol of the Blessed Trinity.

tribunal
PRONUNCIATION: *(try·bew'·nul)*
The church's version of a court. It is here that judges decide whether or not a marriage really exists.

triduum
PRONUNCIATION: *(trih'·doo·um)*
Three days of worship, usually the three sacred days of Holy Thursday, Good Friday, and Holy Saturday.

trinity
PRONUNCIATION: *(trih'·nih·tee)*
This is the greatest of all the truths about God that Jesus revealed. There is only one God, but this God is three persons, really distinct from each other but at the same time completely one.

U

Uniate
PRONUNCIATION: *(yew·nee·ut)*

A branch of the Eastern Church that is in union with the Holy See. It is fully Catholic, but has its own customs and traditions. Eastern churches that do not unite with us under the Pope are called ORTHODOX. Also a member of Uniate Rite.

unjust laws
PRONUNCIATION: (un·just·lawz)
Not all laws are just simply because they are laws. If a law deprives a person of justice or imposes unjust burdens, the law is unjust. If a law doesn't bring the effects intended in making it, it is useless. Christians may, and sometimes have to, oppose unjust laws, inside and outside the church.

V

validity
PRONUNCIATION: (vah·lid'·it·ee)
Certain conditions must be met for the true and valid administration of a sacrament, such as a proper minister, the proper rite, and freedom from IMPEDIMENTS. In many cases, a sacrament may be given validly but not lawfully. This is not usually a thing for most Christians to worry about.

value
PRONUNCIATION: (val'·yew)
To value something is to prize it. When we choose a thing or a way of action as valuable, we must make the choice freely and act on that choice consistently. Our values (choices) pretty much determine who and what we are as well as how we live.

Vatican

PRONUNCIATION: (*vah'·tuh·kun*)

The center of government of the Catholic Church; a nation-state within the city of Rome. The term "the Vatican" is also used to refer to statements or positions of officials in Rome.

veneration

PRONUNCIATION: (*ven·uh·ray'·shun*)

Paying respect by showing reverence to the ALTAR or other sacred place or special person. In the mass the altar is shown reverence by the priest with a kiss and in special cases by use of INCENSE. On Good Friday we venerate the cross with a kiss.

venial

PRONUNCIATION: (*vee'·nee·ul*)

Not deadly (as MORTAL). but hurtful to our spiritual life—our relationship with God and humankind. See VENIAL SIN.

venial sin

PRONUNCIATION: (*vee'·nee·ul·sin*)

A lesser offense against God, lacking one or more of the requirements for MORTAL SIN. Although not deadly in itself, such sin can lead to the deadly and should be avoided by serious Christians. No number of venial sins can add up to a mortal sin, but enough of them could create a tendency where the choice of mortal sin is easy.

vicar

PRONUNCIATION: (*vik'·ur*)

A representative or delegate. A priest may be a

vicar in representing a bishop. The pope is called the Vicar of Christ on Earth.

vice

PRONUNCIATION: (vyse)

The embracing of attitudes or behavior that can lead to sin. Examples are laziness, eating too much, general selfishness.

virgin

PRONUNCIATION: (vur'·gin)

One who has never had sexual intercourse. In a special church sense, one who has deliberately chosen a virginal life for Christ.

virgin birth

PRONUNCIATION: (vur'·gin·birth)

Our belief that Jesus was born of Mary, who remained a virgin before and after his birth. This is seen as a mark of his special dignity as God made flesh.

virtue

PRONUNCIATION: (vur'ɡhew)

A moral and religious strength. The THEOLOGICAL VIRTUES are faith, hope, and charity. Other virtues are prudence, temperance, fortitude, justice, etc. See CARDINAL VIRTUES

vow

PRONUNCIATION: (vow)

An official promise to God that one will perform some action or live in a certain way. The vows of religious life are POVERTY, CHASTITY, and OBEDIENCE. Vows may be made privately or publicly, temporarily or permanently, simply or solemnly.

Vulgate
PRONUNCIATION: (vull·gate)
A translation of the Bible into Latin in the fourth century A.D., attributed largely to Saint Jerome.

water
PRONUNCIATION: (wah·tur)
In the sacraments, water can be a sign of life, death, cleansing, or all three, as in baptism. We die to sin, are born to a new life in Christ, and are cleansed of original and personal sin.

Way of the Cross
See STATIONS OF THE CROSS.

witness
PRONUNCIATION: (wit'·ness)
One who sees or hears a thing occur and then testifies about it. Christian witness means living in a way that testifies to our relationship to Christ. As Christian witnesses, we must be willing to testify to our beliefs even if that means death. The words *Witness* and *martyr* come from the same Greek word, *martyrn*.

the Word
PRONUNCIATION: (thuh·wurd)
The term applies to Jesus Christ who is the Word of God. Jesus tells about God and God's will. The

Greek term *logos* ("word") was important in early theology as a way of explaining the relation of the Father and the Son as the doctrine of the TRINITY was developed.

Word of God

PRONUNCIATION: *(wurd·uv·gahd)*

God's communication to us through any means. Usually this is through the Bible or reflection on it. The term should be used with great care. Christ is also referred to as the Word of God. In Hebrew there is a tight link between word and deed.

work

PRONUNCIATION: *(wurk)*

The necessity for work is seen by some as an outgrowth of Original Sin and by others as a god in itself. Actually, it rates in between. Work is good and necessary, but not if it takes away too much from family life, worship, recreation, and other good and necessary parts of living. Still, work should never be seen as undignified, even in menial forms.

Y

Yahweh

PRONUNCIATION: *(yah·way)*

God's name as revealed to Moses. It means roughly "I am who am" or "I will be who I will be." For general purposes, it means the same as God.